The Lucille Johnson Story

Financial Elderly Abuse Of A Matriarch

The Lucille Johnson Story

By Bernard Johnson

Contents

506 NORTH EAST SKIDMORE PORTLAND, OR 97211

Donna

Your's Truly

Geri   Susie Mae

Lois

David

Introduction

Out of the thousands of crimes committed in the United States on any given day none are more egregious than that of Elderly and or Child Abuse, because these are the most helpless of victims. The criminals that target these demographics are considered the lowest and most vile of all, as well they should be because anyone that abuses an elderly person or a child should be punished swiftly and harshly.

These predators have a variety of abuse methods, physical, mental, verbal, and financial, and or any combination there of. Unfortunately research has shown that Financial Elderly Abuse is the least reported and or prosecuted of all the fore mentioned abuses. The reason being states that it is due to the fact that three quarters of offenders are in some way related to the abused victim which make it less likely to get reported out of fear or embarrassment on the part of the victim.

I write about this issue for a few reasons and they are, (not necessarily in this order), I hope to shed light on this rapidly growing, under reported, crime wave and in doing so, exposing some of the perpetrators and at the same time empower victims and or their love ones to come forward. The pool of potential targets of Elderly Abuse is growing every year because of the high percentage of the population in the United States is at or over retirement age and people are living longer. Citizens with love ones at risk need to be made aware and pay closer attention to them and the criminal element needs to be put on notice that the Abuse of a Child or the Elderly, financial or otherwise is unacceptable in today's society.

I have a more personal reason too as to why Elderly Abuse is an issue to me and why I'm fighting against it and that is because my Mother,(Mrs. Lucille Johnson) fell into that pool and became a target and was victimized by two of her own daughters and grandson, at the age of 84 years old. The full extent of the abuse didn't come to light until she turned 92 years old.

The primary reason I'm writing this book is that I don't want my Mother's Contribution to this society, her hard Honorable work, her Magnificent presents on this earth, and her Touching of so many lives, her own family, and hundreds, if not thousands of others is not lost and or forgotten, as is what her two daughters and grandson would hope happens, because all she was to them was their Cash-Cow, so this is why I'm telling her story.

ACT-I

Should Have, Could Have

It has been said by people that are much wiser than myself that death is a natural part of life, but I submit to you that death is actually the end of life, at least, as we here on earth know it. To loose a loyal friend to death after 30-40 years could be to some just as hurtful as loosing a family member as well. I've lived long enough to experience both, and I've shed tears for the loss of both. Even to this day I shed tears for two of the most Beautiful Women of my life, my Mother and my Wife, may you both rest in piece!!!

On one beautiful summer morning in 1998' when a very dear friend of mine, (Wilburt, aka, Herkey) (may he rest in piece) and I had just returned from having breakfast at the local Land Mark Bar and Grill, (The Overlook) in Portland Oregon, just down the street from my Mother's home. We pulled up in front of my Mother's house and just sat there talking, Wilbur was never short of words. He and I grew up in the same neighborhood just three blocks away from each other, but he was 2 years my junior. We never hung out together as we grew up but we both attended the same Grade and high schools years ago. He and several of his friends would come to the shop where I worked to get fashion tips and I would hook them up with the latest fashions in the late 1960's. Our close relationship didn't begin to blossom until he graduated from college some years later.

Although Wilburt knew that he was most comfortable staying in his own lane which was academia, he had this fascination with the fast lane of life and when he finished college he looked me up. When he came to my apartment to visit he saw that I and a few other of my friends were fully engaged in the fast lane i.e. hanging out at the Night Clubs, chasing women. We would also be gambling, shaking the red card, spending time at the after hours joints, going to the horse and dog tracks, well that intrigued him and he just had to be a part of it. He and I began social-izing from time to time partying and going to the gambling joints and pool hall together throughout the years. In 1973 I was upgrading from a one bedroom apartment I was renting and moving into a 3 bedroom house and he needed a place to stay because he was still living in his mother's basement, so I turned the place over to him, I've never seen a happier man when I handed those keys over to him, that was his first apartment, he was off and running after that and he never forgot what I did for him that day.

Throughout the years I ran into him in a couple of states and up north in Canada one year where he even took me to the tailoring company he was doing business with up there and I had to again give him a few more pointers on the fashion tip, he had the gift of gab, but he had yet to get the dressing part of game in order. Our friendship lasted for decades all the way up until he passed away in 2008 when I than attended his memorial service, I truly miss him because he was a true and loyal friend.

As we sat there in the car just talking he began to confide in me about how one of his sisters had swindled him out of his inheritance and took over the family home when their mother passed away sometime earlier. Because the house was no longer in his mother's name but now in his sisters name she failed to share with him the proceeds of the property. He never said that she abused their mother in any way but he said she was not fair with him. He went on to warn me and suggested that I should make sure that the same thing didn't happen to me. I responded by saying to him, ("Man, there is nobody in my family that would do some shit like that, they know better!") (Wrong!!!). Well, it turned out that I should have took heave and did a bit more investigating into the state of my Mother's property. Had I went and talked to my Mother at that time perhaps I could have minimized, if not prevented what was to transpired Less than 2 year later.

And to let you know just how good of a friend that man was to me, he confided in me too and told me that he had been diagnosed with a heart disease. Then he went on to suggest that I buy a life insurance policy on him, he said (" B, that's what friends are for") I said "Wow!" and thanked him for even suggesting that I do that. But I never got that policy, nor did I think about my Mother's house again, that turned out to be a huge mistake on my part, not getting the insurance policy, but talking to my Mother about her home.

ACT-2

The Migration

———ᴍᴍ———

*O*n the late 1990's my Mother Mrs. Lucille Johnson fell prey to my youngest sister, Bernita Johnson who convinced our Mother to borrow $30,000 using her property at 506 n.e. Skidmore, in Portland Oregon as collateral. At that time all my Mother owed on the property was a $6000 Government repair loan. My mother, (God Bless her Soul), was no match against a street-wise disrespectful child that was hell bent on getting what she wanted no matter what the cost, or how much she hurt my Mother in the process. She knew how to manipulate my Mother as she had done many times before throughout the years but nothing to this Financial degree. My Mother, unwisely did this transaction for her knowing that her other children would have fiercely objected to it.

Mind you, my Mother grew up in the South, she was born in Bryan Oklahoma in 1920 the first of 6 children, 3 sisters, Rudy, Bernice, and, Bertabe and 2 brother's, Joe Fred, and J.D, they were all raised by their mother Annie Lee Hopkins. My Mother's formal education only went as far as the 8th Grade but, she earned her (Honorary PHD) in (Soul Food Cooking) thanks to her mother, and she also (Majored) in (how to Love and take care of her children,) all 10 of them (Unconditionally) which later proved to be her financial undoing beginning at the age of 85.

She worked hard all of her life to raise her children, 6 of them all on her own. And because she wanted a better life for them she knew with her limited education, that she had to work extra hard to prepare for the future of those kids, and herself as well. She was wise enough to know early on in her life that should there come a time or if she lived long enough to get to an age where she needed financial security that she had to prepare herself for that eventual circumstance. Lucille Johnson, my Mother, migrated from Oklahoma to Oregon as a teenager in 1939 with her 2 eldest sons, she was accompanied by her husband, the late Louis Johnson Sr. my Father,(who I didn't actually meet until I was in my 30's, which Is another story in itself).

When they arrived to Oregon they were able to set up residence in the town of Van Port where the majority of the Black population lived just north of Portland. They remained there until 1948 until the great flood there forced them out, she was a survivor of that flood. When the dikes broke in the town it caught everyone by surprise and where my Mother lived was near ground zero. My father was away on the job out of state so my Mother had to get herself and 4 children and an infant out of harms way to higher ground, treading through knee high flood waters for over a mile to get to safety.

By the grace of God my Mother had befriended a woman some years earlier that she would also cook for and the woman owned a two story duplex in north Portland on Page Street. She allowed my Mother to stay in the up stair portion of the property free of charge for a couple of months until my father returned with enough money to catch up on the back rent.

After my father bailed on my Mother some four years later leaving her with now 5 children, myself being the youngest at that time, she had to step up her game. So she did just that by using her skills as a prolific (Soul Food Cook) to find a job in that arena to began providing for her children. She started out working at one small Soul Food restaurant owned by a gentleman by the name of Eddy Collins Sr. that was located on N. Williams Ave. After cooking there for him a year or so she moved on to cooked for a different Cafe called The Blue Ribbon, now owned by the same woman that helped her in a few years earlier, we all called her Aunt Ruth. It too was also located on N. Williams Ave. My Mother would go to the job in the mornings and work through the lunch hour, than she would come home and cook for her own children, she would return to the job for the dinner hours. She did that for several years until being approached by a young up and coming visionary businessman by the name of Paul Knolls who recognized and appreciated her cooking skills, he made her an offer to come and work for him at one of his establishments for a better paying position. He hired her to work at The Flamingo, one of his busiest nightclub/restaurants on north Russell Street, aka, (The Low End) aka-(Red Light District) in north Portland as well.

Although her Soul food was second to none she also became known for her baking skills as well, Cakes, Sweet Potato Pies, Banana Pudding, and her signature Peach Cobbler. She had people ordering her cakes and pies on a weekly bases and they would come to her house to pick them up. She worked there at the Flamingo for several years serving people from all walks of life, doctors, lawyers, gamblers, store owners, pimps and prostitutes, she was cooking for the whole town and she for the most part enjoyed doing it. One evening a regular customer of hers brought in a few of his friends in for dinner, she cooked for and served them. A week or so later one of the men came back with

9

his wife, and after serving them the man handed her his card and told her to call him on her next day off. She did just that, that gentleman asked her if it was alright that he meet up with her at her house on n. e. Skidmore, she agreed. Once they arrived at the house, he and his wife, sat down with my Mother and over coffee and sweet potato pie. During that sit down he went on to explain to her that he needed a cook for the company for which he was managing and that he thought that she would be the perfect fit for the job. The gentleman ended up offering her the ideal position as head cook with full benefits cooking for the children at Perry's Children Center located in s. e. Portland, where it remains to this day. Although my Mother was doing alright there at the Flamingo, this new job opportunity meant that she could work set hours and be home by five and not have to deal with the sometimes, drunk, loud and belligerent customers there. Perry's Children Center was just what my Mother needed and enjoyed doing because now she would be cooking mostly for children and the staff members at this beautiful complex where there was no alcohol served and she was surrounded by children. There at the Center she cooked for hundreds of children over the many years she was employed there and she remained there at Perry's for over 15 years when at the age of 69 she retired with all the bells and whistles, the children and staff there all loved her and really hated to see her leave.

My Mother Lucille Johnson was a Woman, (in my bias opinion), that was as close to a perfect Mother as one could be. Not because she showered us with gifts or gave us everything we wanted, quite the contrary. What she did do was kept a roof over our heads, kept us modestly, yet comfortably dressed, mostly in second hand clothes, and put food on the table, which in the days before and during my adolescents, that wasn't an easy task, especially for a single mother of six. What she did do as well was install in us what it meant to work for what you wanted and to be independent. Many years before she landed her last three jobs she had to find a way to earn money to feed her children and that meant she would wake us up early, (us being) my sister Lois, and I, at 4:30 or 5 o'clock in the mornings, and we would walk to the bus stop and catch that big yellow bus. And it wasn't that yellow bus like the ones they have today that takes the children to school every day, No, it was that 10 year old, out of service, raggedy yellow bus that took us to those bean and strawberry fields to pick those beans and or strawberries to earn money.

Although the harvest time was in the summer months it would still be very cold early in the mornings. l still recall those cold wet ass beans hanging from the vines, many of them covered with those little black bean eating bugs that would squish blood in my hands as I picked the beans off the vines. I also remember arriving to the fields where then we were assigned a row or two of beans to pick, and those row seem to me like they were one or two city blocks long and I was only 9 or 10 years old when I started and my Mother and my older siblings had been there, and done that for years so it wasn't nothing to them.

We were provided with 10 pound buckets to put the beans in as we went down the row and when they were filled we were too provided with what I called Croaka sacks that we would dump the buckets of beans into until the sacks were filled. After the sacks were filled they could weigh anywhere from 50 to 70 pounds or more each and I recall my Mother dragging those heavy ass sacks down the rows as we picked the beans. And then at the end of the row she and my sister Lois would many times drag those sacks one by one down the field to where they were to be weighed. I would often see my Mother carry the sacks all on her own, I always marveled at the strength that beautiful woman had back in those days. She was the hardest working woman I had ever seen and I watched and learned from her what it was like to work hard for what you wanted and needed, my father was nowhere around, it was all on her! But that was how I earned the money to buy my school clothes for years, that was my summer job. For those and other reasons she should have been treated with honor and respect, and not have been violated in the way that 3 of her children/grandchildren laid upon that true icon of a woman.

ACT-3

Ebony, The Unforgotten

———∽∞∾———

$\mathcal{A}$s was mentioned earlier Bernita, was successful in convincing my Mother to take out this loan on her house so, she obtained the application for the home loan and delivered the papers to my Mother for her to sign off on. Bernita made sure that all of the bills and correspondence pertaining to said loan went to her address in Vancouver Washington because she was to be responsible for making the $500 and change payments. Now my Mother was now at the mercy of what turned out to be just the first of a few parasites that were waiting in the wings for their turn to take advantage of an aging woman, a pillar of the community. The other parasites just so happened to be one of her other daughters, Geraldine, and her grandson, Terrol.

I became aware of the loan my Mother took out on her home for Bernita some years after the fact and in doing so I knew it was just a matter of time my Mother would live to regret it. So it was no surprise to me that in 2003 my Mother was notified by way of Bernita's daughter,

Ebony, that there was trouble with the loan payments and that the loan company was calling in the note and that my Mother's house was in foreclosure, which turned out (Not) to be the case.

Ebony was the child that Bernita lost to the system when she was just 3 or 4 years old because of Bernta's drug use. That action by the state broke my Mother's heart when she was taken away because my Mother was for the most part raising her. My Mother had this extraordinary ability to love all of her children/grandchildren, no matter what they did, and there were many of them. Ebony, although she was removed from the home at an early age, she was no exception. My Mother would always think of Ebony, it was almost like, if not, an obsession with her. She would every year for many years bake a cake on Ebony's birthday in the month of February counting the years she was away, shit, she didn't even bake a cake for me, unless I requested one, and my birthday is in February as well! She never lost hope in believing that she would someday see Ebony again. Then there came a time some 13 years later when Ebony turned 18 in 1997, Bernita went online and with the wonders of technology allowed her to reach out and touch her. She was then in a short period of time able to reunited with her, (an event, in my opinion, should have never taken place at that time.) Unfortunately it turned out that my concerns were well founded.

Ebony had been raised and educated by a loving and caring couple, (the Huber family), they are known for taking in children that were placed in the system for various reasons, and of all nationalities. They reside in Amity a small town in Oregon, less than 100 miles from Portland and they took Ebony in and raised her as if she was their own child.

Some years later on one of my trips from Portland to Sacramento, I took Ebony to her former home in Amity and at my Mother's request I thanked the Hubers personally for taking such good care of Ebony.

While I was visiting them there in their small, yet comfortable home, I couldn't help but notice all the photos of the many children that they helped educate over the years. I dubbed it, their (Wall Of Fame Of Graduates) that these unselfish people had allowed in their home. There was as many as 25 perhaps more when I was there some 10 years ago. The Huber's are to be commended and recognized for their work in helping, and guiding all of those beautiful children I saw and the others since, that I've not seen.

I've lived long enough to see how life has a way of throwing curve balls in peoples lives, and no one is immune, and trust me, I've had more than my share of curves thrown at me, but not all of them were strikes. In the game of life, unlike the game of baseball, fortunately for most people three strikes doesn't always mean you are out. But in the case of Ebony, she was thrown her first curve ball at a very young age when she was born to a mother such as Bernita. The second curve that was thrown to her was being removed from a loving family and grandmother in particular. The third curve ball life threw at her was indeed a strike and hit straight across the plate. That strike was when she was unexpectedly contacted by her mother, because this turned out for her to be the worst, (daughter, mother) reunion story of its kind on the books. After said reunion Ebony came to Portland shortly thereafter and she was no longer that young child any more, she had grown up to be this 5'7 black beauty, educated, and a class act, everything Bernita was not. One would think that Bernita would be this proud and appreciative mother to see how well her first child had turned out, (Wrong!).

Bernita, being the mental case that she was couldn't appreciate the wonderful work and attention that the Hubers put into grooming this beautiful child, preparing her to go into the world to be this productive and successful citizen. It became apparent in a short period that Bernita was very jealous of her own child and her accomplishments and she

15

couldn't stand the fact that now she had to be, in her mind, reduced to be standing in her daughters shadows.

At the same time however Ebony's reemergence made my Mother the happiest Grandmother on the planet. When she laid eyes on Ebony for the first time in close to than 15 years, her prayers had been answered. Tears of joy flowed all over her face because she saw everything in Ebony that she so hoped Bernita would have turned out to be. Unfortunately the happiness my Mother felt was short lived because Bernita felt the need to set forth a plan to prove to her that Ebony was no better than she, it was as if Bernita didn't want to see my Mother happy, which was nothing new, she always felt that way, it was just the way she was wired.

When Bernita found Ebony on line, Ebony had just graduated from High School with honors and adding several academic and sport scholarships to her credit to some of the top Universities in Oregon and some from across the country as well. Ebony was on her way to doing great things with her life had she not been side tracked by the very person that gave her life. What followed in the months and years to come played out like something out of a V C Andrews, or Stephen King novel. What Bernita wanted to do was, well, scratch that, frankly, speaking, I don't know what that warped minded Bitch wanted do! All I do know is what she did, and for starters she misguided her daughter and placed her in an environment that completely derailed her from the goals and aspirations she was so keen on achieving after graduating from high school.

ACT-4

The Degenerate

———⁓〰⁓———

To understand these sad series of events that were to be played out, I have to take you back and explain to you how over the years leading up to the present how things got out of hand and continued to manifested its self into this feeding frenzy, my Mother being the main course. When Bernita became pregnant with her first child Ebony she was the last of my siblings living with my Mother, which gave her the forum to begin to take advantage of my Mother, that included talking to her disrespectfully and mistreating her unabated. Once Ebony was born my Mother's fears of knowing that Bernita was not mentally stable enough to have, let alone, raise a child was of grave concern to her. My Mother so hoped that she was, at her age, had finished raising children especially after Geraldine had finally moved out just a few years earlier and took responsibility for her children. Now here she finds herself again having to take charge in making sure that her new grandchild would be taken care of properly, because that is the kind of woman my Mother was. She knew that if she didn't step in and help raise her beautiful granddaughter, in her home, Ebony would not have never had a chance.

The reality of this situation is that although Bernita was this unstable individual she was in no way stupid, she was actually a very smart person. She was smart enough to know that my Mother was fed up with the disrespectful and nefarious way in which she was being treated by her. She knew too that the next step was that my Mother was just about to put her ass out of the house and into the streets where she belonged. Bernita, knowing my Mother as she did, she knew that she had to come up with away to secure her residency there at 506 n. e. Skidmore, (in her mind), her solution was to just, get pregnant, have a baby, my Mother would never put her out then. Well this most selfish, yet brilliant move, again, (in her mind) worked out just as she planned. The little Devil on her shoulder had to be high-fiving her and encouraging her to do more because she had just pulled off a triple play. She had a child she didn't want or need, she secured a place to live for years to come, and in the process acquired a permanent night time baby sitter while she ran the streets, in my Mother. My Mother was now, again thrown back into overtime grandmother duties, something she really hadn't signed up for.

During the subsequent years things were less than ideal for my Mother, she was in an impossible situation, she had the choice of putting the bitch out and pray she did right by that child, or let the bitch stay in the home and just deal with the disrespect and abuse for Ebony's sake. There was no way my Mother was going to entrust Bernita with her granddaughter living out on her own. Over the next 3 or 4 years Bernita continued her unstable behavior until finally CPS (Child Protective Services) became involved and eventually removed Ebony from the home, simultaneously breaking my Mother's heart in the process.

Bernita, was just this out of control unfit and failure of a mother, the removal of Ebony from the home was not because of anything my

Mother did, as Bernita tried to guilt my Mother with, but because she was just this misfit and unfit of a mother. It may sound as if I'm being hyperbolical in my description of Bernita, but the fact of the matter is, at that point, she was just getting started, fasten your seat belt!

Mind you, my Mother had successfully raised 8 other children, none of whom showed any signs of mental disorders, or retardation, before Bernita came along. I say 8 because my Mother was blessed to see 9 of her children grow up to adulthood. Sadly she lost one of her daughters in the summer of 1954 when a drunk motorist struck and killed my sister while she was crossing the street on her way to the neighborhood grocery store right around the corner from where we were living on north Knott Street in Portland Oregon.

Her name was Susie Mae and I remember that pretty little girl after all these years and I also recall the memorial services vividly to this day as well and I was only 3 years old at the time, she had to be 6 or 7 when she was killed. From that time on my Mother would on every Memorial Day, and or on Susie Mae's birthday find a way to get out to the cemetery which was 20 miles away from where we lived to place flowers on her Baby's grave site. That went on for many years and what else went on for those same years was that my Mother would walk to her jobs every day to make sure she could keep us housed and fed. Having to try and raise a child like Bernita was her biggest challenge out of all of her children and she didn't see it coming until it was too late. It was like a woman after raising several somewhat normal children only to realize that, there is something wrong with this last one but not being able to put her finger on it. So she just for the first 8 or9 years of Bernita's life my Mother handled her pretty well with little problem and it was uneventful for the most part.

So as time passed the only means of transportation available to her back then was catching the bus or calling a taxi cab, but she chose to walk instead to save money, and she saved for years. She was determined to save enough money for a down payment on a house for herself and her children.. It took her close to 8 years but she finally had enough money saved to put a down payment on a house, which was a huge accomplishment and a proud moment in time for her. Once she bought that house on N.E.. Skidmore she continued to catch the bus and or get rides from friends and family to work for years until one day she made it up in her mind that she no longer wanted to depend on anyone, anymore to get her back and forth to anywhere.

My Mother decided that she would learn how to drive, she was well into her late 40's. One day she approached me and asked me to teach her how to drive, I was floored, yet excited for her. At that time I was a Junior High school and had my first car, a Black 1959 Chevy Impala that I Dubbed, (The Bat Mobile) and that is the car that she learned how to drive in. It took awhile but less than 6 months my Mother had her Driver's Licenses which was a major accomplishment for a woman of her age and limited education. The excitement and pride that she exuded as she walked out of that DMV office after she passed that drivers test was second only to that day 6 or 7 years earlier at the closing of the purchase of that house on north east Skidmore, and I was there for both milestones, I was so happy for and proud of her. This had opened up a new world for my Mother, she for the first time in her life could get up and drive herself to work, or anywhere she wanted to go. The freedom that came along with jumping that hurdle gave her the confidence, and a feeling which was life altering, one could see the joy that it brought her, I was so proud of her.

So now we then had to find a car for her and she wanted a big car, because she was afraid of small cars, and she was a plus-size woman. It just so happened that one of her friends had a 1962 Cadillac Coupe in her garage that her father had once owned, she sold it to my Mother.

She was now able to drive herself back and forth to work and visit her baby Susie Mae whenever she wanted to, it was like she had been set free. She enjoyed the freedom of driving herself around town in that big Caddy for a few years. It wasn't until her health issues began in her mid-80's that she was unable to drive herself around anymore. Even then, again, she had myself or one of her other children go to and place flowers on Susie Mae's grave site and this went on until she passed, she never forgot her baby girl, and now she is laid at rest just a few feet away from her just the way she planned it. This is just one of many examples and a testament to how much love that woman had for her daughter and all of her other children.

Johnson Wins 100th Fight

Dempsey Is In Audience

JACK DEMPSEY (center), selected the fight between Louis Johnson (left), of Hickam and Roosevelt Hamilton of the Marines as the "Fight of the Night" at last week's special matches held at the Bloch Arena.

Louis Johnson of Hickam won the hundredth fight of his amateur career last week at a special "Jack Dempsey" card attended by the Marine Maule at Bloch Arena.

The local featherweight decisioned Roosevelt Hamilton of the Marines to gain the victory.

The fight between Johnson and Roosevelt was selected by Mr. Dempsey as the "Fight of the Night."

In other contests involving Hickam fighters, Robert Lucas light-heavyweight, drew with Otha Biggs of the Navy, and James Barrow, light-welterweight, lost to Ronald Coleman of the Marines by a decision.

Coach of the Hickam boxing team is A/1C Shelby Nash.

LOUIS HENRY JOHNSON

ACT-5

A Mother's Crown Jewel

*M*y Mother's first 2 sons went on to graduated from High School then they both went on to serve in the Arm Forces back in the mid-50's and served Honorably for 20 years respectfully and retired from there. In fact her second son, Louis Henry Johnson went to the 1964 Olympics in Tokyo Japan representing the United States Air Force in boxing. Although my Mother knew that he did that, what she didn't know because she wasn't computer savvy, is that he is memorialized on the World-Wide-Web, for his service to this country. She was already proud of him, and had she learned that before she passed away at the age of 94 years old, I don't know if she could have been any more prouder of him because the truth-be-known, he was to her (The largest Jewel in her Crown) out of all of her children.

She never knew that I was aware of that and she never said that, but I knew it, and to me, he earn that position, as he was a True Soldier and a Great man in every since of the words and he is missed by all!

My Mother out lived both of her 2 eldest sons by 6 years, Willie Roy Johnson, the son that along with his wife, Alice, were the ones that co-signed for my Mother to get the house at 506 N.E. Skidmore. He was the first of her sons to pass away after a courageous bout with cancer while living in Denver Colorado and was survived by his 3 beautiful daughters and 1 son. I recall, it was a week or so before Roy's passing my Mother called me to let me know that he was sick but she didn't say how sick. It was probably because she didn't realize he was on death's doorstep because he never told her how bad he felt and he was still at home. Then again she might have just thought because she knew that he and I were estranged and had been for many years. In fact she knew too that it had been close to 30 years that he last spoke a word to me due to a real estate business deal gone bad (the house he was living in) that he failed to pay me for. My Mother, being the diplomat that she was never did ask me about the details of what her first born Roy, and myself, her third son, pertaining to that property but she was torn seeing that it had came to such a point between us, again, her unconditional love for all of her children came into play.

A week later she called me crying while telling me that Roy had past away, and it was as if I could feel over the phone how sad she felt. As she was explaining to me the cause of his death I could here in the background my uncle J D's voice as he walked in to the house, it was then that she told me she would call me back. She didn't call me back until the next morning and her words to me were, "Bernard, now I know you and Roy were not on speaking terms and I know too for some reason he really didn't care for you but I need you to put that aside for now and do me a big favor, I need you to fly up here and help J D drive over to Denver to attend Roy's funeral, will you do that for me? I'll pay for your ticket, please!" Little did she know is that had I known Roy was in his last days I would have gladly few over to Denver to comfort him, he was my brother. Of course I would have liked to have been paid the money he owed me for the house but the fact of the matter, I at one time I loved and trusted that man. It saddens me to know that man died hating me, all because of money and that he felt it was out of his reach to repay me for what I'd done for him. One of which was put him in a position to become a pillar of the community all those many years ago. But it was a no brainer, of course I caught a flight to Portland the next day, paid for it myself. After going to the house to hug and talk to my Mother for an hour or two just talking about her first born, my uncle J.D., his best friend, and my sister Lois, who loved her big brother Roy big-time, and I got on the freeway that afternoon, destination, Denver Colorado to attend his funeral, my Mother's health prevented her from taking that trip.

Once we arrived to Denver we all stayed at the house that I purchased some 30 years before and nothing in that house had changed since the day I left there all those years ago, and I mean nothing. It was as if I had took a trip back in time, there was no cable, no internet, and all the same furniture he purchased was sitting just as I left it. The only thing that I saw that was out of place was the King–size French Provincial bedroom set I sold him when he moved into the house was moved from the Master bedroom to the guest bedroom across the hall. The next day I went through those familiar dresser drawers and the only thing I found in them was a dozen pair of beautiful Men's hosiery, that I was going to put on the market and had given him some 25 years before that he had never worn, sill in the package I designed. That man really hated me, I'm surprised he kept the bedroom set.

We stayed there for a few days and laid Roy to rest after which our brother Louis felt the need to accompany us on the drive back to Portland so he could try in some way comfort our Mother. Her seeing him would for sure make her feel better because it had been awhile since she had.

He stayed up there in Portland with her for a week or so consoling her, I had to get back to Sacramento, so I couldn't stay that long.

There is nothing like a thousand plus mile road trip that can really bring people together, or not, as in getting to know someone. That was the first time that my sister, brother, uncle and I were in a situation where we could engage in such a way. Its truly surprising what one can learn about a person under those circumstances. In my case, in those hours of our travel I grew closer to and appreciated all 3 of them even more, all in a different way. Not only as my relatives, but more so as who they were as people and what they really meant to me, and that trip back to Portland with my brother was meant to be. Although he and I took a road trip 20 years earlier from Denver to Oklahoma City and in doing so we had time to bound as brothers because he was 12 years my senior and he was away serving his country while I was growing up, but that trip was a bit different, it was just he and I, but this last trip with the four of us was special as well. We all talked, agreed and disagreed on many subjects during the long trip, but what we more importantly talked about on that trip back to Portland was our Mother. Including what she had to be going through at that moment in time, being unable to attend her 1st sons funeral as well as the sacrifices she made and what she did to get us to where we were in life at that moment. There was no way anyone of us could have fore seen it but, life was about to throw my Mother another curve ball that would result in her loosing another child.

It was less than two months after our road trip, I was awakened with a phone call from my sister Geraldine, she was hysterical and in tears, telling me that our brother, Louis was dead. Louis Henry Johnson Jr, who too fathered two beautiful granddaughters for our Mother has died under suspicious circumstances in his home in Denver Colorado. So now my Mother now had two sons that both passed away in the same year, 2008 less than 60 days apart. What are the odds of that happening? The lost of Louis hit me in a way I really can't explain, I wasn't only heart broken, shocked and angry, I was also afraid. I was afraid for my Mother and what effect this unbelievable turn of events would do to her and how she would react hearing such devastating news, she was 88 years old and on dialysis 3 days a week. After I received the news I knew what I had to do, I immediately made reservations for myself and my daughter, Da'Narsha to fly to Portland to see about my Mother.

I realized then why my brother Louis felt the need to travel to Portland with us to see about our Mother. My daughter and I stayed with her for a couple of days consoling her because it was being said to her that Louis had committed suicide and she was not believing any of that. We then flew on to Denver to find out just what happened to my brother. The days before we arrived in Denver it was being said too that my brother's death was a result of an home invasion gone wrong.

Once we landed and settled in the town I went to his house where I was then informed that the circumstances surrounding his death had changed. It was now said that he shot and killed himself in an apparent suicide, (Really!) I didn't believe that either! My brother Louis was not a rich man monetarily, but, he was rich at heart and loved life. He was a successful man and had no reason to commit suicide. This man raised two beautiful, highly educated, and successful daughters, as well, and was financially secure enjoying his life, what reason would he have to commit suicide? I think Not! That man I just recently drove across country with us for hours showing no signs of depression, in fact he was the life of the party all through the trip. It was strange to me that the investigators never gave his wife Shirley a (GSR) gunshot residue test, they just took her word for it, that he shot himself. I guess the detectives on the case fail behind on a few episodes of CSI Miami, because had they did been current they might have given her one, I bet Lieutenant Horatio Caine would have seen to it that she got one. I've made several attempts over the years to get the autopsy report with no success. At the funeral home I asked the people there if they had a copy of the autopsy report and they told me yes, but at the request of his wife Shirley he was not to release a copy to me, I thought that was a pretty suspicious request by her. My brother's death was ruled as a suicide, neither I, my Mother, nor any of my siblings ever excepted or believe those findings, even to this day.

After the huge two day service honoring him we flew back to Portland to try and comfort and support my grieving Mother once again. How my Mother, Lucille Johnson survived and handled that double tragedy at the age, 88, was nothing short of miraculous because, she herself had just begun taking dialysis treatments 3 days a week in that year and was unable to travel to attend either of her sons funeral services. So in all, my Mother out lived 3 children and 3 grandsons and still she never waivered in her trust and faith in her God. She was a true Rock Star and she was not finished yet!

ACT-6

The Confrontation

—∿∿—

Getting back to this troubled child Bernita, who by and up until the early 2000's had become a master at manipulating and misusing my Mother over the years. My Mother was torn and actually afraid of this Bitch, to the point that she wouldn't even tell me what was going on in the home while this Bitch was living with her in fear of reprisal. That was because she knew I never stayed in Portland for any length of time and when I would come in town to see her she knew I would be leaving any day so she would act as if everything was alright. Bernita pretty much had her way with my Mother while she lived there with her, and it continued until she finally moved out. Before she moved out however there was a times when I should have taken more action against that disturbed Bitch but I didn't realize just how bad it was. I do recall one incident, I had just came back from one of my trips in the early 80's and I came over to spend some time with my Mother and Bernita was there. As we were just sitting there in the living room watching television and talking, I can't remember just what was said but, all I do remember is my Mother was sitting on her couch while Bernita was sitting on the floor next to her and I was sitting in my Mother's chair across the room. As we were engaging in conversation my Mother said something to me and after my Mother spoke that Bitch Bernita turned to her and told her to shut up or be quite or something to that effect. Before I knew it, I was out of my Mother's chair and over there where Bernita was sitting on the floor with my hand around the collar of her neck about to slap or choke the shit out of that bitch. But, my Mother screamed out my name so I caught myself in mid-swing, and just told that Bitch, "if I ever hear you talk that way to my Mother again, or if I get it from a third party your ass was mine!" The domestic violence laws were not as tuff back then so I had no problem putting my foot in her ass, about her disrespecting my Mother, In my face plus I had plenty of money and it would have been no problem for me to make bail.

I was just in total shock that the little Bitch thought it was alright to just blatantly disrespect and talk down to my Mother in such a fashion, in or out of my presents and think that I wouldn't reach out and touch her ass. My Mother didn't just keep Bernita's abuse towards her from me, she wouldn't tell any of her other children 3 of whom were living near her and at the time I couldn't understand why. Looking back on it I came to understand that my Mother would rather take the abuse from Bernita rather than to tell any one of us because she was in fear of one of us getting hurt or going to jail trying to defend her because she knew that Bernita had violent tendencies and would gladly take one of us there. That Beautiful Old woman had so much love for her children she was still protecting us at her own expense when we should have been protecting her from this abuse. My Mother indeed felt some guilt, but more over she also felt fear and lived with those feelings for years, not only because of Bernita's tactics but, because she came to the realization that this child that she had (bore, adopted, and or found on her door step),(which I believe is one of the ladder,) turned out to be this Mentally disturbed, Psychopath and had no clue as to how to deal with her. Bernita was like this kind of mutant living in her mist and my Mother didn't know how to get rid of this Bitch. And what my Mother didn't know too, was that Psychopaths have no remorse or empathy for the pain they cause to other people, they might mimic empathy at times but they just don't have the capacity to truly do so.

ACT-7

Lost And Turned Out

———∿∿∿———

$\mathscr{N}$ow, Ebony, being sheltered most of her life made her the perfect mark for a street-wise predator such as her mother Bernita just as my Mother was. What happened next showed the true evil in the mind of a Psychopath and how it works. Once Bernita saw just how much joy, love and admiration my mother showed for Ebony, she set out to destroy that joy. Unfortunately but needless to say sadly, Ebony never went back to that award winning couple in northern Oregon, (The Hubers),the ones that set her on the trajectory to success. Instead she listened to her mother and stayed in Vancouver Washington with her for that summer and by summer's end Bernita had managed to maxed out all that child's credit cards and in the process and turned that beautiful child out to the worst drug she could find, Crack Cocaine, (her own child). My Mother had no knowledge of what was happening to her granddaughter during her stay that summer because it had yet to come to light. Now that Bernita went through all of Ebony's assets, it was now time she figured out how to get more money to finance their drug addiction, not just for tomorrow or the next week, but through the future. So she had to put a plan in place to get it from somebody, who was her next target?, my Mother.

Bernita used the fact that my Mother was so proud of Ebony's education and accomplishments she found a way to exploit it in a way to convince my Mother to borrow money on the house to finance her education by telling her that Ebony had inspired to get off drugs and she had been off drugs all summer ever since Ebony came back into her life. Bernta then went on to tell my other of her plan, and the plan was that she and Ebony would both enrolled and attend school the coming up semester in Corvallis, Oregon, at Oregon State University.

My Mother was not aware of the fact that Bernita didn't need money from her to get back in school and that there where student loans available to her to do so, and Bernita knew that. Nor did she know that Bernita had already taken out loans years earlier and failed to repay any of them, thus, disqualifying her for other loans. Had my Mother known that I doubt she would have took out that loan for her. But my Mother wanted so bad to see this dysfunctional child of her's to make something of her life, and being that she brought Ebony with her to make her pitch, knowing Mother adored and respected her, it was hard for my Mother to say no, (she was out numbered), so she went for that Con and gave in to it. I want to note that Ebony had no clue that her mother Bernita was and had been for the years while she was away mistreating her grandmother, now she was an unwilling participant of this deception and a victim as well.

Once Bernita received the check less the payoff of the $6000 lien on the house, she had something north to $20,000 at her disposal. Bernita had never in her life been close to being a $20,000 Bitch, she had no clue as what to do with that kind of money, nor did she have the means,

34

or the discipline to take on such a responsibility and repay such a debt. Of course she went on to buy a car, supposedly to get back and forth to School, (something that never happened). She proceeded to just Fuckoff the rest of the money on drugs and partying, with her daughter and others, the fact of the matter is she never got clean over that summer as she told my Mother she had done. The car was, to no surprise, repossessed in less than a year or so later and she soon found herself back walking in the streets doing what she has always done before to get money. This including, but not limited to ruining my Mother's credit because she had obtained and knew all of my Mother's information which made it possible for her to get credit cards in my mother's name as well. Back then there was no FICO score it was called, A-1 or AAA credit and that's what my Mother had before Bernita got a hold of it. She was also able to find a way to borrow money off of an insurance policy that my Mother had on my sister Donna. These and other ways such as having Ebony filing false insurance claims, (slip and falls) was just one part of her on going schemes. She even convinced that child to physically injure herself so that she could sue another insurance company. This Bitch was on a tear which allowed her to keep up with the payments on my Mother's house for a couple of years until she finally hit rock bottom taking her once beautiful daughter Ebony down with her. It was also said that she was able to somehow borrow another $10,000 on the house without my Mother knowing it, (I have not been able to confirm that).

Bernita was able to keep my Mother in the dark about her deception for so long because she resided in Vancouver Washington, just across the bridge from Portland. My Mother was under the impression and or just praying by this time that Bernita and Ebony had truly enrolled and began attending college, she had no way of verifying it. It wasn't until 7 or 8 months in that she no longer saw that Bernita driving the car that she bought that my Mother began to realize that she had been bamboozled by Bernita, my Mother had to be shaking in her boots. The next indication was that Ebony's appearance and demeanor began to change i.e. she had began loosing weight, and she started to display signs of one that had a nervous condition, she couldn't stay still. These were traits my Mother had become oh so familiar with in years passed with Bernita and they again began raising their ugly head with Ebony as well. So now my Mother now had two Crack-heads to contend with, a total nightmare!

ACT-8

From Boy To Man

—————ᗰ—————

*D*uring the years, 1978-1990 I was traveling back and forth to overseas destinations and I would be away sometimes for months at a time but I would always send my Mother money every month not caring about what she did with it, because she was my Mother, unlike her 2 eldest other sons. They would not send her money because their reasoning was that if they sent her money she would only help Bernita with it and they were not ok with that. But she was my Mother and I learned years earlier that not looking after your Mother and making sure she was alright was a recipe for disaster and could have grave consequences. How do I know this to be true, you might ask? Well, let me tell you how I know it.

The days of my spiritual enlightenment began in 1971 when my Mother held a family photo day, all 9 of her children were in Portland at the same time which was a rare event. And it just so happened that I just returned from a trip to Canada and I was looking forward to having one of my brothers co-sign on a car for me. Being this young naïve soul I didn't know what the responsibility one would have to take on in signing their name on to a contract for a person with questionable ability to repay. I think I had a couple thousand dollars, which was a nice piece of change for a person to have, cash, back then, or so I thought. So first I asked Louis to do it, he wasn't comfortable with doing so for various reasons. I then approached Roy with a slightly different pitch, he too gave me his reasoning for *not wanting to do it. It was at that moment I understood that I was* on my own in this endeavor which turned out to be the best thing to do in the long run after all.

After the photo session we all engaged and gorged in the fine Soul Food my Mother had prepared for the occasion after which everybody was just kind of relaxing around in and outside of the house. So now it was time for me to go and try to get this car that I so badly wanted and needed. I had enough money to buy a car but, I didn't have enough money to buy the car I really wanted without having a co-signer, because I didn't want just any car, it had to be a Cadillac. While my Mother and I were in the house alone, she in the dining room and I in the living room for a moment, I didn't see her, so I went into my pocket and I pulled out my money to count it and she walked in on me while I was doing so. When she saw me counting it, the look on her face was one of surprise, all she said was, "Oh baby, can I have one of those, please?" (It was all hundred dollar bills). And what I said to her in response haunts me to this day. What I should have said was, ("yes Mother, here take 2 or 3"), but what I did say to her was, ("No Mother, I have to buy a car with this money") and I put that money in my pocket and walked out of that house on that woman not giving her not one of those $100 dollar bills that she asked me for.

That selfish act proved to be one of the worst mistakes I ever made in my young adult life and it haunted me for a long time, because I can't even to this day believe that I told that Beautiful woman who worked so hard to raise, feed, and house me that she couldn't have some of that money! So when I walked out on her that day I had a friend come to the house and he took me to a few car lots to see if I could purchase a car. After the third attempt and being told for the third time that because I was this 20 years old kid and without a co-signer, I needed more money, before they could sell me a car. So now I'm angry and frustrated so my friend and I went to the club to have a few drinks and try and come up with plan D, because, A, B, and C had failed.

Plan D turned out to be that I would go to the After hour Joint located on northeast Union Ave. now (Martin Luther King Boulevard) that was ran by my well respected O.G. friend, his name was (Sailor Boy), where he served drinks and we could play cards and shoot dice, (he too died prematurely, some years later, well before his time, in a violent fashion by the hands of a young Hater that had no respect for his elders!) I figured I would take a couple of hundred dollars in there and parlay it into the extra money I needed to satisfy the car dealer so I could drive off the lot with a car without a co-signer. Well, it didn't take long for that couple of hundred to change from my hands to another's, in fact I went out to my friends car and got another few hundred. And the beat went on from there because it quickly became clear that plan D stood for Disaster, because it wasn't even 3 to 4 days later that I ended up back at my Mother's house, in her basement, (I had a house in North Portland and was behind on the rent that I now couldn't pay and didn't want to face my landlord) with little or no money, no car, because I had went into the streets, drinking and gambled off pretty much, if not all, of that money!

After staying in her basement for a day or so recovering from the hangover of the past few days feeling stupid, I dragged my broke ass upstairs to fix something to eat, (my Mother's food). As I was preparing my meal my Mother walked into the kitchen and she sat down in her favorite chair at the table next to the window. I was standing in front of and facing the stove and when I turned towards the table where she sat and looked into her eyes, the look on her face as she focused on me was one that I'd never seen nor will I ever forget. When she spoke to me, it was in a tone that I had never heard from her either. The calmness, the sincerity, and her disappointment in me, was so overwhelming it was all over her face, she knew I was broke! Listening to her voice as she read me the Riot-Act as it was coming straight from her heart, and it hit me like a ton of bricks. She never raised her voice, she never curst me, she never even told me to get out, (and she would have been justified in doing so), but by the time she got through with my ass, she made me feel so small, I broke out of that kitchen and out that front door so fast, like a little puppy with his tail between his ass.

On that day my Mother, (borrowing a lyric from the Icon, Stevie Wonder, from his 1976 hit 2-CD, (Song In The Key Of Life) a song titled (Joy Inside My Tears), when he sang, "Asking Permission to lay something heavy on ones head" well my Mother laid several heavy things on my head that day, (without) asking my permission I might add, the most heaviest one was when she took me back to the early days of her family life. She went on to tell me about how she, her sisters, brothers, her mother, and her father, (when he was around), had so much difficulty in putting food on the table in those days. She, her siblings and their father, George Hopkins had to get up every morning and go to the cotton fields to pick cotton to earn money. How my grandfather, and my uncle J.D. would have to go out hunting for squirrels, possums, rabbits and how they all had to also grow their own vegetables to put food on the table. Her point was, and I got it, was that during those times there was a family bond that couldn't be broken, the survival of the family depended on it, what one had, all had, and whatever little money that came into the home was shared by all, that was the way they lived. It was then, and only then, did I fully understand why my Mother and my uncle J.D. were so close, he did the hunting, she, her sisters, and mother did the cooking, as they grew up together during the most trying times of their lives, they had a bond that would never be broken!

She also went on to tell me about how in 1955 she took in her 15 year old younger brother, Joe Fred, after he and a friend hitched-hiked and train hopped all the way from Oklahoma City to Portland to get away from the terrible living conditions there. Although see was taking care of her 6 children in a small 3 bedroom apartment she made room for her baby brother, he was family. The moral of the grilling she was laying on my head was that, nothing comes before family and that was the way they survived back in those days. (And by the way, I was so mesmerized and dumfounded at what she was saying to me coupled with the wisdom there in, I never did get a chance to eat that meal I prepared that day.) I was a 20 years old, irresponsible kid on that day with no sense of direction, I never went back to that house I was renting either, I lost everything in it. But that too was the day I grew up and became a Man!

ACT-9

Home Coming

When I finally returned to my Mother's house several months later to see her she was sitting on the porch, as I was pulling up in my car, I noticed that she was looking and wondering who it was pulling up on the wrong side of the street parking in front of her house. When I stepped out of the car she seen it was me, she was happy to see me but she really didn't want to show it. As I was walking up the stairs towards her she just couldn't help herself, she jumped out of her chair and met me at the edge of the porch with a big hug and kisses, I too gave her a big hug and kisses as well. I then went on and apologized to her for being less than a man to her on that day months earlier. After which, I reached into my pocket and pulled out a envelope and gave it to her, I still remember the very words that came out of her mouth at that moment when she opened it, and counted what was in it, all she said was, quote, ("a thousand dollars, thank you Lord!") unquote, with tears in her eyes. She took that money and used most of it for a down payment on a car, because the car she had was pretty much a none starter and about to shut down on her. It just so happened, and lucky for me that my timing was just right on that day because during the hugs and tears we both shared I couldn't help but smell that Folgers coffee brewing, and the familiar aroma of her smothered potatoes settling on the stove, the homemade biscuits freshly baking in the oven along with the famous spicy patty sausage that you could only get from Chuck's Meat Market, located on north Williams Ave. resting on the stove as well, all coming through the screen door. There could not have been a more appropriate segue, so we went into the kitchen and I sat her in her chair at the table where her famous canned Pear Preserves that she canned over the summer before sat. I then went on to fix her and myself plates, but not before I fried a couple of eggs, (over medium) the way she liked them and then we sat and enjoyed a Pure Soul Food breakfast, as we talked and sealed our unbreakable bond forever.

Ever since that day my Mother never had to worry about money, because if I had money she would never go without or want for anything as long as I had it, and for some reason God saw fit to Bless me for many years in that area which allowed me to provide for her. I recall there were times when I would take her 30, maybe 40 thousand dollars for her to hold for me because I wasn't using banks at that time. And when I came back to retrieve my money it was never short, but even had it been I would have been ok with that because by that time my understanding of the magnitude of what that Beautiful woman had done, not just for me, but for all of her children in her life became so profound to me, it was well beyond money. She was my Mother and had spent any of that money, she deserved to have it! My Mother was not a stupid woman and she knew I was living in the fast lane and she had no fear or problem with holding my money for me because she knew it was not drug money. I Loved, Trusted, and Honored her, and still do to this day although she is no longer here with me.

Several years later when my Mother retired from her last job at Perry's Children Center, I had just flew in town and I went over to the house to see her. It just so happened I couldn't touch any money that day because I was waiting on my Banker at Credit Suisse to transfer me some funds to a bank there in Portland. Mother was in the dinning room, and I was in the living room on the phone talking to a friend and she overheard me asking him if he had money he could send me but he was unable to do so. So when I hung the phone up she was standing right there in the dining room and she overheard the conversation. So I just turned to her and asked her, jokingly, because I never asked her for money, I said "Mother do you have any money?", not knowing that she had just received a large retirement check. That woman was so happy to say to me, and with a smile on her face, "Yes baby, how much do you need?"

She then proceeded to go into her purse and gave me what I asked for, it wasn't but a couple of hundred, but it pleased her to no end to let me have it, That too was another one of those moments I'll never forget about my Mother because that was the same room she asked me for that hundred dollars and I turned her down some 15 years or so earlier, (needless to say, that never happened again).

I've kept a copy of that family photo we took in 1971 with me in a briefcase where ever I went for a long time. I would take it out and look at it from time to time because it in some strange way it kept me focused, when I came across it, and even to this day it has a place in my living room. The most ironic thing about that photo is that it was just in the last few years or so when I looked at it and I realized that the 2 girls sitting on the 2 ends of that couch (Book Ending) my Mother were the 2 girls that would ultimately be the two that would betray her in the worst way and in my opinion contribute to and send my Mother to her premature demise, all over money! My Mother was on par to live to be

100 years old, and I truly believe that she would have, had it not been for those two girls and her grandson!

When you look at that photo and look at the Johnson Family, that girl sitting on the far left of my Mother is as much as a Misfit as one could be, and I reiterate, I truly believed my Mother adopted or found that child on her door step. I have a very good memory of times gone by, and I can't think for the life of me remembering my Mother being pregnant with that child! Just look at her!

ACT-10

Secret Revealed

$\mathcal{My}$ Mother was a proud God fearing woman and she had a lot to be proud of. She was also a high ranking member of the Eastern Star Religious Organization and was Loved and well respected among her peers there, she also mentored several of the up and coming members. I sent her on trips with the Organization over the years, on a couple of them they went to The Bahamas one year, and another year I flew her to Hawaii with them, and those where some of the most exciting times of her life because she was able to, after working so hard in her life these were ways to get away from and take a break from the likes of that sick child of her's Bernita. I can only imagine how much pressure my Mother was under carrying around that secret about what she had done for that undeserving, disrespectful, troubled child. Once she began to realize just how grave of a mistake she had made in doing so it had to have taken a heavy toll on her having to deal with that over the years. Coupled with the fear of what could really happen if Bernita failed to live up to her responsibilities, and what her other children would think of her when and if they found out. It breaks my heart to think about how she must have felt, she was in her mid-80's dealing with that kind of stress. Her children and grandchildren should have been taking care of that Beautiful woman, not misusing her!

Although Ebony was by this time a full blown drug user and addict, thanks to her mother, Bernita, she still had the presents of mind to go to my Mother with what she thought, and that was, that my Mother was about to loose her home because she knew Bernita had received a letter from the loan company demanding the back payments. She knew that foreclosure proceedings would be the next step and that meant my Mother would have to come up with the total balance of the loan, which was somewhere close to $25,000. She didn't have the letter, Bernita had it, and she was missing in action when Ebony came to my Mother. She was no doubt on one of her insurance scams and or some where trying to smoke up all the Coke in the town.

But in reality all my Mother needed to do was to come up with the $1500 or so to catch up with the 2 or 3 payments that Bernita had failed to pay because the house was not yet in foreclosure nor was the company calling in the total loan. It just so happened that the day Ebony came to the house with this devastating news my sister, (Geraldine Johnson, aka, Gaines, aka Jones, aka Gardner) was there. It is not clear to me if Ebony knew that the loan my Mother took out for Bernita was to be a secret from the rest of her children, or at this point considering the state of mind she was in, she no longer cared who knew it because it had become an (all hands on deck) situation. Geraldine, (God Bless Her Soul, because she really needs it!) was living just a few blocks away from our mother, just getting by, as we all were at that time and for her to hear this news from Ebony, trust me, I know, it wasn't sitting very well with her. Geraldine was at one time, in her own right an attractive, loving, person and if she cared about you she was a fierce and loyal protector, a person I would want in my corner when the chips were down. I truly love her although when we were growing up together in that house we fought like cats and dogs as did a lot of siblings.

But when I moved out at 16 years old to go to live in my sister Rosizean's, basement because she lived right across the street from the High School I attended, Jefferson High, it seemed as though the relationship between Geraldine and I grew stronger, in fact I know it did, we just needed our space.

Moving Out

―〰―

osizean is my Mother's eldest daughter, beautiful woman, she stood about 5'6, with dark shoulder length wavy hair, with a personality to match, and a child that my Mother was also very proud of as well for many reasons. She was the first of her daughters to graduated from high school and then went on nursing school, got married and bore her three beautiful grandchildren. She always kept a job and she would always come and check on our mother on a daily basis because when she moved from the nest and married she only lived a few blocks away.

Being that she was the first girl of the family she saw firsthand and learned from mother how important it was to keep a job and take care of her children and she was indeed a super mom and great sister as well. And a few years later after separating from her husband she moved just 1 block from our mother and after that but, before she moved across the street from the high school in 1966 she lived about 5 miles in the other direction from my Mother's house on Borthwick Street in north

Portland. Rosizean too was able to land a part-time job working for Mr. Paul Knowls at the Flamingo Bar and Café on the night shift as a Cocktail waitress/Bar Maid. She would need someone to come over and baby sit for her two eldest children a few nights a week, and guess who that someone turned out to be? Right, yours truly, and that was right up my alley. As soon as that phone rang and I heard it was Rosizean on the other end I knew she was calling my Mother to ask if it was alright for me to come over, I was out that door in a flash, I ran that five miles in record time, every time. This was my time to get away from Geraldine's crazy ass, and plus I wouldn't have to wash the dishes on my dish nights, which pissed Geraldine off Big-Time, and I loved it!

Geraldine would probably have been Rosizean's first choice to baby sit for her but, they at that time didn't really get along that well. I know too that Geraldine grew to be very jealous and envious of her big sister. I think it was because she felt Rosizean had one up on her because she had gotten married before she became pregnant or soon thereafter and living in her own house. Unlike Geraldine who was still in high school when she got pregnant with her first child which made her feel some kind of way less then, in my Mother's eyes, which in reality not the case. My Mother loved Geraldine just as much as she loved all of her other children. Of course my Mother was disappointed and angry with her because Geraldine was a bright student doing very well in school and college bound and that life altering derailment through my Mother for a loop. My Mother knew what challenges that faced her young daughter, and abortion was not an option. Plus Geraldine had to take care of her own first child, Terrol and she was in such an angry place in her life at that time which she had to come to grips with before she could move on. It took some time before she, Geraldine, came to her senses and realized that her anger towards her big sister was misplaced and it wasn't until her son Terrol came to an age where she was able to return to school and in the process she achieved her own academic success was she able to see that. It didn't take long after for her to swallow her pride and reach out to her sister apologetically, making piece with Rosizean. By her taking that step she soon became aware that having done so, it had its rewards and advantages, because Rosizean, who was loved by all and had a lot of friends in high places in that town.

After I moved out of Mother's house and in with my sister I never returned to live with my Mother and from the time I moved out nobody could ever say anything bad about me to Geraldine, she was like my own personal gate keeper.

ACT-12

The Late 1960's

———∼∼∼———

*I*t wasn't long after living in my sister's basement maybe a year or so I landed a job at the busiest men shop (Lew's Men's Shop) in north Portland on the (Low-End) as it was called, I was this young high school student working at one of the finest Haberdasheries in Portland. I was working in the heart of the (Red Light District) where everything was going on, and I mean everything! At that time the town was on fire, money was everywhere and the people were spending it every day and night. Lew Gress, the owner, my mentor, was this handsome fellow of the Jewish persuasion standing about 5'9, with salt & pepper hair, and chiseled features, to me he stood 10 feet tall, that's how I looked up to him. Lew didn't know it at the time what hiring me would mean, but then again, maybe he did know exactly what he was doing because he was a Brilliant businessman.

That man, Lew, started out going door-to door selling his wears, i.e. suits, shoes, and hats, just to name a few, to the predominantly Black population, he extend credit to them back in the 1940's in the town of Van Port before the big flood. He went on and grew his business to be a local land mark and the place to go if you were a man, young or old and wanted to dress in the latest styles in the City of Portland Oregon, because he had it all, and he literally built that shop from the ground up. By him hiring me was just one of many brilliant marketing strategies that he used in all the years he was in business. In less than a year of him hiring me I had the shop jumping off the hook with students from no less than four high schools in the city flooding into that shop to do business, especially during the holidays, all because he hired me, this was a demographic Lew had never tapped into before 1967.

But in full-discloser, before he hired me, Lew knew my sister Rosizean, because she had an account with him at the Shop for years because she would buy clothes for her husband on the regular. Lew grew to love, understand, and respect the people to whom his business foundation was built on. And as a result of that he also grew and acquired a taste for good O'l Southern Soul Food. He only had to walk a half a block from his Shop to the Flamingo where he would do breakfast, lunch, and or dinner, to satisfy his taste for it at least 5 days out of the week, cooked and served more often than not by none other than my Mother, Lucille Johnson. Lew was just one of the many executives and business owners in and around the City that frequented the Flamingo to enjoy my Mother's Southern culinary skills.

After working at Lew's for a little more than a year, I moved out of my sister's basement and into a rented a one bedroom apartment and that little space felt to me like my own penthouse, except for that that it was on the ground floor. I was finally out on my own. Things could not have been going better for me. I was just a Junior in high school, had a job, and on my way to the top of the world, or so I thought. One night after getting off work I was to meet up with a couple of friends at a Dancing In The Street Party at Boisie Grade School on Freemont Street in north Portland, which was just 2 blocks from my apartment. So after showering and changing my clothes I walked from my apartment to the school, when I arrived there I noticed the people walking off the playground headed towards their cars, the party was shutting down, I was too late. While standing there gazing at all the beautiful young girls I missed mingling with exiting the party I noticed my friends headed to the car they came in. It was a white top red body 1965 Thunderbird owned by my friend Ray, so I joined them and got into the back seat of the car. We left the party and drove down Freemont Street a mile or so to the gas station located at the corner of Union Ave.(now MLK) and Freemont Streets to get gas. As my friend and owner of the car Ray, he has since changed it to (Ya'Sin), went into the station to pay for the gas my other close and dear friend, Byron Branch, (may he rest in peace) and I were sitting in the back seat of the car just talking. While sitting there I glanced across the street and saw another close friend of ours, Henry Bryant as he was pulling his car into Mc Donald's parking lot, which was kiddy-corner to where we were, plus I was hungry. As I reached forward to get out of the back seat I simultaneously, out of the corner of my eye saw Ray approaching the driver's side door after paying for the gas, all of a sudden gunshots rang out.

All I remember after that was that I buckled backwards, and hearing Byron crying out after the 38 caliber bullet that struck me in the back of my neck had shattered the rear driver's side window splashing glass into his eyes. As Ray was opening the door of the driver's side to get in, he too was shot directly in his back. After the shooting stopped the fourth passenger, my friend and a bail bounds man, Eddy Magee, the only passenger that had not been hit by the gun fire had the presents of mind to go around the car and help Ray into the passenger side door of the car, put him in and then he got into the driver's seat and drove us to the hospital. Little did he know was that the car was on a flat, a bullet had hit one of the tires as well, but he, and by the blessings of God got us there in time, and we all survived. I think that might have been the first Drive-by-Shooting in Portland Oregon's history, or for sure the first one in the late-1960's.

Once we arrived to the hospital the least injured passenger, Byron, was the one making the loudest cries for help from the car and in the hospital as well. Eddy came around and assisted Ray in the door of the hospital, as Byron passed them up and got in the door first, I sat in the backseat I'm watching this unfold. It then occurred to me, I'm the only one still in the car, I know I should be on my way into the hospital too, but nothing was working. I was then hit yet again, only this time it was with the frightening reality, that I was at that moment paralyzed and couldn't move and no one knew it.

After sitting there for a moment bleeding out it became clear to me that I was on my own, so I had to literally will myself to rise and get out of that back seat, it was a 2 door car, and thankfully in the haste to get Ray out of the passenger side of the car Eddy left the door open. Once I finally made it into the hospital doors the nurses took one look at me right there in the hallway and then they rushed me straight into the operating room. The resident doctor there at the hospital had to call in a Specialist in to do the delicate surgery of removing the bullet from my neck because it had lodged so close to my spine. After several hours of being in the OR I was placed in the ICU room to recover. A day or so later when I came to, it was like I was surrounded by 3 angles at my bedside, the first one I saw standing next to me was my Mother, she didn't know whether to cry or smile, the second was my High School sweet heart, Barbara, the mother of my first daughter La' Shon, she was standing on the other side of the bed holding my hand and the third one was Geraldine standing at the foot of the bed, smiling at me, I was truly happy to see them all.

After spending seven days in the hospital recovering they released me and Geraldine was there at my apartment for me to help change my bandages almost everyday for the next week or so whether I needed her there or not. She stepped up for me back then showing again that she really had love, concern, and compassion for me and I never forgot it.

But let me tell you how shrewd a businessman Lew Gress was. After I was released from the hospital he came to my apartment to check on me. He walked in and saw that I wasn't really bedridden, we sat and talked for a few minutes about the business because I had been missing in action for well over a week. On his way out, he said, he called me Bernie, he said "Bernie, you know the 4th of July is this coming weekend, do you think you can come down to the Shop and just sit at the door, you know its going to be real busy for the next several days, I need you there." That man was really about his money, and I loved that, and respected him, because he hired me when I so needed a job and simultaneously help sharpen my Fashion skills. That was knowledge that had it not been for him I would have never had, something that has carried me throughout all of my adult life, so you know I showed up to the job that following Friday, bandages and all, for him.

ACT-13

Changing Of The Minds

can only speculate as to what happened to Geraldine's love and compassion that she showed through the years towards me, and others and especially my Mother. I can only contribute that to greed and the love of money and wanting so bad for her children to have what she couldn't herself give them, no matter what the cost or who got hurt in the process, including her own mother. Money and greed has a way of altering some people's thinking and actions in ways that are beyond imagination.

Years earlier when I was having things my way I wasn't just taking care of my Mother, I would see about my sisters as well. I would send or bring Geraldine money also gifted her for her children. I even went so far as to loan her money to help her and her down and out men friends she chose to be with. I really loved her, she was my sister, and she had my back if I needed her or not. But she had this (Bad Boy attraction thingy going on), but I tried to be understanding and just let her know I still loved her, I even gifted her with a 24k Gold neckless even while she was with one of those looser ass Bad-Boys and she wore it proudly for years. She was my sister and to this day, I love her but, I hate how she lost focus and how she and her son abused my Mother for financial gain. The Fast-Lane was not one that was for her so it was short lived, but she was a people person and she became a part-time barmaid/cocktail waitress for awhile, making decent money doing so as well, following in Rosizean's footsteps. Her failed relationships turned out to be somewhat of a blessing to her because out of a few of them she bore three children in the process, Terrol Johnson, Steven-?, and Arleta Gaines. All of her children turned out to be pretty decent and productive off springs and that was mostly due to the fact that our Mother helped raise 2 of them in her house on Skidmore most of their young lives. It wasn't until my Mother went out on that limb and took out that loan for Bernita and Geraldine became aware of the upcoming default/non default of said loan did she get her inspiration to put her devious plan together to take my Mother's house and abusing her in the process.

It was no surprise that Geraldine was capable of such anger because her passed acts displayed how enraged she could become. She even lost a couple of high paying jobs in her early years due to violence against her co-workers at the work place and she never recovered from those incidents. Unfortunately for my Mother Geraldine's children didn't fall too far from the tree and became willing co-conspirators in the plan to take my Mother's home and selling their souls in the process as well.

Terrol, her son, also went on to serve for a few years in the Armed Forces, and he too made his grandmother proud just as her 2 elder sons did. My Mother had a lot to be proud about when it came to her children/ grandchildren, but not so proud of them that she would have given any (one) of them her home. Teroll and I had a very close relationship as well, we traveled to some of the same Foreign countries, he being in the Military, myself just being an independent World traveler and I loved that man as if he was my own son. We did several things together business wise, one case in point, one year when he was stationed in South Korea and I was living in Japan I would have him send me merchandize to Tokyo, Ell Skin briefcases, hand bags, and luggage, I would then turn around and I would sell them to my Japanese associates and friends there. I respected and trusted that man with my life, literally. I had him as my beneficiary on my insurance policies, but it turned out that I was betting on the wrong horse, that man truly broke my heart.

Geraldine, being the person that she is has always been protective of her children, which is understandable, but she took it to another level which was that she would even betray her own Mother to see that her son was financially secure. Had she not been such a violent person when she was in the workplace she could have kept one of those high paying jobs and been able to save her money as my Mother and other hard working people of her generation did and purchase a home of her own for her and her children rather than having to stoop to swindling my Mother out of her's.

When Ebony came to the house that day telling my Mother the dreaded news that she hoped and prayed she'd never hear, Geraldine was right there hearing it as well. Knowing Geraldine as I do, just the thought of our Mother giving that disrespectful Bitch, Bernita any money, let alone trusting her with over 20 plus thousands had to have just infuriated her and I'm sure she only seen Red because of it. I can only imagine what she had to say to my Mother in private after hearing this outrageous shit. Geraldine, was living just a few blocks away from our Mother and could have at that time used a few thousand dollars herself but she never thought about asking our Mother to take out a loan on her house for her even though she may have needed the money. So for her to hear that Bernita, not her, was more worthy of my Mother's financial support did not sit well in her mind and I totally understand and agree with her on that point, Bernita should have been the last person my Mother should have trusted. Geraldine felt as if my Mother had betrayed her, and that sent her into a revenge mode and she decided to take it out on all of the family, all she cared about then was her and her son from that day forward, our Mother be Damned!.

Geraldine was not the only person in attendance when Ebony came to tell my Mother the bad news, my uncle J.D, my Mother's brother was also there. Now, he and my Mother were as close as a brother and sister could be and he is a retired Long Shore man with deep pockets, and just looking at him and my Mother side-by-side, you would think they were twins but my Mother was a few years his senior. There is nothing that man wouldn't do for her, he too was hearing this shit for the first time as well, and happy about it, he was not. But this time, the numbers Ebony was throwing around, $23,000-$25,000 was out of reach even for him in this case. He too wasn't educated enough to know just what and how to get to the bottom of this situation, plus he also was angry that his sister would go out on a limb like that for Bernita.

But had he known that the loan company really only wanted the back 3 payments of $1500 or so, he would have bailed his sister out, reluctantly, but he would have, no question about it. Even had he not given it to her, he would have let me have it so I could get her out of that mess. I know this because J. D. and I were also and to this day very close and we too did business together. He has always been my Go-To-Guy over the years, when I needed a two or three thousand dollar short term loan I would call him, and then I would call Donna, she would then meet him at the bank or at our Mother's house and he would give it to her. She would then send it to me, the man has never turned me down, so I know $1500 or$2000 would have been nothing for him to help his favorite sister catch up with the back payments she needed on that loan to get out of her situation.

After a few days had passed, with no response from Bernita, and watching my Mother sitting around with nowhere to turn, Geraldine decided to put her devious plan in motion. She went down to the finance company on behave of my Mother to do some damage control of her own. Mind you, Geraldine too was a very street-wise dame in her own right and knew a financial opportunity when she seen one, and this was one.

Being that my Mother is in belief that her house was going to be lost in a month or two and she was this 83 year old woman and in fear of being in the streets had to be excruciating for her, yet Geraldine kept her thinking that. So when she did go down to the loan company with her son Terrol (who had just recently returned to Portland and homeless as well living with my Mother), the company let them know that all they wanted was just for her to catch up with the delinquent payments and all would be fine. Geraldine never told my Mother that but, what she did tell her was that what Ebony had said was true, but that she had the solution to this problem and that was, let her son Terrol put the house in his name. She told her that by putting the loan in his name under his G.I. loan the payments would be less than what she was presently paying and she could get Bernita out of her business for ever. This sounded like music to my Mother's ears, and like the answer to her prayers, she felt now that she could trust her daughter Geraldine and her Military Veteran grandson to get her out of this terrible situation that Bernita had placed her in. They told her that she could use her Social Security checks to pay the loan off not having to depend on Bernita's ass anymore, her problem would be solved. In a perfect world that would have been an ideal and a beautiful ending to the terrible ordeal my Mother was going through the last few years, (WRONG!) Because what was lurking around the corner for her was far more sinister than she or anyone could have imagined.

ACT-14

Battle Of The Greedy

When Bernita finally surfaced some week or so later stating that she was in the hospital or some crazy ass shit, she more likely was on a week long Crack mission. Anyway, now that she was back she was hit with the realization that she was no longer in charge of the responsibility for making the payments on my Mother's property and that her key to the house no longer worked. So now she had no free access to the house and Terrol was now in control, that bitch flipped out. Then Terrol promptly called the police on her and had her removed from the premises, her reign of terror over my Mother was over, her ass was out. What else Bernita was reminded of at that time was that she had to finally come to grips with the fact that Geraldine, not her, was the more street-wise woman and now in charge and that there was a new sheriff in town.

Geraldine just couldn't wait to get back at that bitch's ass, because she so much wanted to put her in her place and this was the opportunity of a life time to do so. She already thought that she was ten times sharper then Bernita, and as it turned out she was also ten times more greedier as well. Now she had the power to prove it and the fact of the matter is that there was never any love lost between those two from the get-go. What she and her son Terrol had in fact done is what I called a (Ghetto Version) of a corporate takeover.

After Geraldine and Terrol went to the finance company to obtain the necessary paper work for my Mother to sign and brought them to her to do so, she also brought along her own personal (notary) who just happened to be her sister-in-law for the signing of the transfer of Deed. The papers I obtained from the Court House in Down Town Portland, the first one, dated 2003 (Statutory Warranty Deed) states that my Mother, "Lucille Johnson, Grantor Conveys and Warrants to Terrol Johnson, Grantee, the following described (real property free Of Encumbrances" Really! My Mother could not have understand it if she read it, let alone knew what it meant! Plus my Mother could not have written her signature that straight on the line of that document if she had a (Rubber Stamp Signature Pad) to do it with! Frankly speaking, that signature looks to me more like it was forged by the Notary rather than written by my Mother! It is suspect in nature at best, and criminal at worst!

It goes on to state (The True Consideration for this Conveyance is $75,000) which meant that my Mother sold her property to Terrol for that $75,000. My Mother never seen a penny of that money. My Mother was not selling her home to Terrol, nor was there any money exchanged from him to her for that purchase. My Mother never gave her home to Terrol either, all she was told was that the house would be transferred to his name until the loan she took out for Bernita was paid off. She was to start making the New Loan payments off of his G.I. Loan, she was just trying to get out from under that $20K loan Bernita stuck her with, that was all. On the next page, dated the same day, the (Statutory

Bargain And Sale Deed) was Notarized by the same Notary states that "Terrol Johnson, Grantor, conveys to Lucille Johnson, Grantee, with, True consideration of the conveyance as $00.00." Well, can I get a little help here? And I've had a few years of College classes under my belt, and even I need help with this". It goes without saying, my Mother was desperately in need of help with this shit because little did she know was that she was surrounded by greedy and heartless people that she herself brought into this world and raised and they were out to get her at all cost.

The conspiracy, fraud, and deception began to take shape. At that time the loan had been paid down to somewhere in the range of $20-$25,000 or so, I'm not by any means a mathematician but, the court records show that the loan paper that Geraldine and her son, Terrol presented to my Mother to sign was in the amount of $75,000, my Mother was not aware that she was signing off on those kind of figures, and surely she was not aware that she was signing any papers that stated that she was (selling) her home for any amount! Had she known what they were doing to her I know she would have called me before she signed those paper, if, she was the one that signed them at all.

They too Bamboozled that desperate old woman. Those figures were much more than the loan she took out for Bernita and way too little for the property value of her home at that time, which had to be no less than $200,000 a far cry from what she owed on the loan she was trying to pay off. This amount gave them $40-$50,000 over and above the balance of the loan to do with whatever they wanted to do with, and none of it was to help my Mother, she never received a dime of that money. One would think that once they received that $50,000 over and above what my Mother had authorized, at least one of them would have come to her and said, "here Mother/Grandmother, take a few of these thousands and pay off some of your other outstanding bills and get some of this pressure off of your mind." They not only didn't do that, they never even told her that they borrowed the extra $50,000, and never told her, "you just sold me your house for $75,000". (Really!) My Mother was under the impression that her Air Force Veteran Grandson was doing what a grandson who loved his Grandmother would do, not expecting anything from the woman that raised him, knowing it was just the right thing to do.

They never even bought her a coat, a pair shoes, or paid a bill for that Beautiful O'l Woman with her money. The sad part about this deception is that my Mother would have gladly approved of some additional monies had they made her aware of it, they didn't even respect her enough to even asked her if they could do it. My Mother was scared out of her wits of loosing her home and being put in the streets as they told her would happen. She didn't know it at that time but she was having to now look at two more people for years to come that she thought she could trust and they turned out to be Parasites as well. She never said to Terrol, "grandson, I'm giving you this house, this is now your house because I put it in your name", nor did she say, "Terrol, I'm selling you this house for $75,000", none of that ever happened! In fact she never knew about the $75000 transaction that took place in 2003 until 2013 when all of the other unauthorized loans were discovered.

ACT-15

Uncounted Payments

My Mother then began paying on the loan out of her Social Security checks in 2003 which was in the neighborhood of $500 every month thinking that this was the only amount needed. She had no clue that it was just a portion of what the total payment was and that they were paying the remainder because they never let her know that they had borrowed more or how much more it was, so she and I continued doing so for over 9 years. After those years passed we are now under the impression the $25,000 loan was pretty much paid off after all that time.

But what was really happening was that every month Geraldine or Terrol would get the payment from my Mother so that they could send the actual amount to the loan company because the actual amount of the payment was never known to her.

This went on for all those years with my Mother and myself thinking all was well and back to status quo, and she would have all this behind her in a couple more years. But the fix was in, they had pulled off the biggest scam of their little bitty lives against the aging Matriarch of this family. They are now feeling real proud of themselves.

When this deception first took place I was living in San Francisco, and I would talk to my Mother on a regular basis and I would also talk to Geraldine and Terrol on the regular as well. Looking back on it, I can understand why my Mother might not have wanted me to know what was going on. It was because she just couldn't quite bring herself to doing so because of our relationship, she perhaps felt she had betrayed me in some way. But as I mentioned earlier, Geraldine, and her son Terrol, and I were real tight as well and I would have expected if not both, but at least one of them would have called me and told me what Bernita had done to our Mother, nor did they let know what they were planning to do, not one call from either of them informing me did I get, Why? Because they knew if they had told me what Bernita had done and what their plan was, I would have came up with that little ass $1500 my Mother needed and that would have foiled their plans to take my Mother's house. I found out a month after the fact the deception had already been executed by Geraldine and her son Terrol. I drove up to see my Mother a month after they transferred my Mother's deed into Terrol's name. When I got there Terrol was not, and I didn't see him for a day or two after I arrived.

While he is enjoying his success in having transferred my Mother's home into his name, a property he hadn't worked a day for, or paid a dime for, then he takes up permanent residency in 2 of the 3 bedrooms upstairs, feeling pretty good about himself. When we crossed paths after he returned to the house, I remember vividly, we were on the stairway in the house, I'm going down, he is coming up, he stopped me half-way and made it a point to greet me, and tell me, quote ("Hey B, I just want you to know, it is not my intention to take Grandma's house, anybody that's willing and able to help me pay off this loan, I'm cool with that") unquote. Now I'm thinking the man is telling me he wanted me or one of my siblings to help pay off that loan to hurry up and get the house out of his name, so he can go ahead and buy his own home with his G.I. loan.

It didn't occur to me at the time but later it came to me, why would he need anyone to help pay off a loan when my Mother was already paying it off, then I thought, maybe he meant, to pay it off faster. Shortly thereafter I moved to Sacramento Ca., its only a 8 hour drive from Portland so now I could come to see my Mother pretty much every month. When I drove up I would bring her a few dollars as I always done and a bit more towards the house payment. The times I might not get up there I would make sure she still got a couple hundred by mail, and I continued doing that for years, and through the years I would bring or send Terrol money as well. I still didn't know he had borrowed that extra 40 or $50,000 on the house, because he never told me. I'm just trying to help get him off the loan as to his request so that my Mother could be made whole. This is the same man that when I got my retirement check in 1999, I gave $4000 for a business venture when he was living in Oakland Ca., just a few years earlier, before he went to Portland to do my Mother.

This 40-$50,000 secret played out for all those years as Geraldine and her son keep up with the payments without a problem because of my Mother and myself contributing. I say secret because the only people that knew about it was Geraldine and Terrol, or so I thought, because I found out later that Geraldine had been telling some of her closest friends, Debra Smith and Dedra Barron, aka (DeeDee) and a few others, that my Mother's house was no longer her's, but now belonged to her son Terrol. She nor he ever expressed those sentiments to me or any other of our siblings, or my Mother, throughout all the years it

73

was in his name, it begs the question, why not? Before I got that bit of information there came a time in 2012 when our Mother's health was in decline, when David and I were taking measurements of the porch of the house to determine how much lumber it would take to build a lift for our Mother. During that moment Geraldine just happen to call at that time to check on Mother as she often did, she just ask me what I was doing, I told her, we were taking measurements for a lift, (keep in mind, nobody in the family got the memo that Terrol and she considered the house to be his) the greedy bitch responded, " well did you let Terrol know what ya'll were doing?" My response to her was, "No, and why would l have to tell Terrol anything about what we were doing, we are doing this for Mother and why did you even ask me that?" she then said, "well just out of respect" I then asked her, "what do you mean by that?", she just kind a laughed it off and asked me to put my Mother on the phone. The timing of that incident was significant for a couple of reasons, for one there was no reason for me to tell Terrol anything because he was actually standing right there while we were taking the measurements, he knew what we were doing. Secondly, I vividly recall a phone conversation just a few months earlier with Geraldine while our Mother was in the hospital battling yet another case of pneumonia. It wasn't so much what she said during that call, it was more so the stoical tone in which she was expressing herself. I had just returned from the hospital visiting Mother and she was recovering just fine and then the phone rang, it was Geraldine. She asked me " how is Mother doing" I told her she was going to be home in a day or two. She then said, "well Bernard you know mother is 92 years old and we might just have to except the fact that she might not make it this time." I replied, "she'll be fine and she is coming home soon! And I'm not ready to make that call, nor should you!" and I just hung the phone up on her. That conversation took place in June of 2012 and it angered me big-time because it was as if she was saying, our Mother can't live past 92 years old, but my Mother proved her to be wrong. The subsequent phone call when she asked me about whether we talked to Terrol about the lift was in September of that same year 2012.

The question I have about that call is why when I asked her " why should I have to ask asked Terrol about the lift" Why didn't she just simply reply, (Because that is his house, that's why!) Oh, trust me, she really would have loved to have said that to me, but she couldn't fix her mouth to do so. At that time in November 2012 my Mother was struggling, she had just beaten another bout with pneumonia once again, going to her dialysis treatments as usual, yet she was hanging on. She needed so badly to be upstairs in her bedroom where she hadn't been in years and to have access to a walk-in tub so that she could soak her aging body but her will to live would not allow that strong woman to give up.

And it wasn't three months later in February of 2013, the records show that Terrol, that greedy parasite borrowed/refinanced another $125,000 more against her home and didn't use any of it to help get the life prolonging amenities my Mother needed. And again my Mother didn't know anything about any of the loans, nor did she received any of the proceeds from them. What kind of sick person would do that to their mother/grandmother, it's just unfathomable!

ACT-16

The Preacher Man

—⟋⟍—

his conspiracy against my Mother was the just one of more than a few similar acts of (Financial Elderly Abuse) cases that took place in Portland Oregon, between the years 1996-2010, that I became aware of, my Mother's was probably not the most costly, but one of the few in which neither of the perpetrators were ever held accountable for, nor prosecuted for.

Another such incident took place between those years with another friend of mine, I'll just call him, (Rolls). His grandmother, we all called her NanNa, was one of the most classiest Elderly women I've ever met, she also had the most beautiful head of long gray hair, and it was all her's. When she past away she left Rolls and his brother her home and other assets. She left her wishes in a will but the problem was that Rolls's younger brother was not the sharpest tool in the shed. When their grandmother past, not knowing what to do, and being in shock, when their mother got to Portland after getting the news of her mother's passing Roll's brother just gave her the keys to the safety deposit box at the bank. Rolls would have never given his mother the keys or anything else had he been there.

Rolls was out of town on the east coast when he received the news of NanNa's passing and he immediately made reservations to get back to Portland. She loved him Big-time, as did he love her. The problem was that it took him a day to get there from the east coast, his mother was only a couple of hours drive away from Portland and she was able to get there before Rolls could. His mother was the only child NanNa had and they were and had been estranged for many years and this was why Rolls and his brother were raised by and living with their NanNa which is the reason she made the will out to the boys, and not their mother. That box contained all of NanNa's jewels, and there was a lot of it, legal and personal papers, and a copy of the will as well. It goes without saying, Roll's mother never produced the will or any of the contents of what was in the box to my friend Rolls and she went on to exercise her (sole heir status) and filed a claim as such. She and her 3rd son that she did raise while living in Seattle (a banker) wasted no time in applying for and taking out a huge loan on the property. The loan was somewhere in the neighborhood of $150,000, (successfully, I might add). These actions were taking place without the knowledge of Rolls because he and his mother too were not on speaking terms for many years and never seen eye-to-eye on anything. She had no intention of letting Rolls know about her plans to borrow on the house or that she was going to sell the property.

The only thing that saved Rolls and his brother from loosing their entire inheritance was that his NanNa had a brother, Curtis, living with her at that time and he had a copy of the will she gave him to hold or he just found it some years earlier. The other problem was that NaNa never filed the will so it wasn't on record. But once the Uncle Curtis realized what was going on and he saw that the next step was that his ass too was about to be put out into the streets with nowhere to go he then miraculously produced a copy of the will. Fortunately for Rolls and his brother the this revelation was what put a halt to all proceedings that Rolls's mother was engaged in, which was that she was in the process of selling or taking out another huge loan, the (A coup de grace) on the property.

Seeing that my friend Rolls needed help, because after several attempts to hire an attorney to take his case, unsuccessfully, I might add, I sent him to my attorney, Mr. Beck and after a short battle with his mother he was able to regain the property that his NanNa intended for them to have. Rolls however never did recover any of the contents of NanNa's safety deposit box, nor the cash in her bank account. I do have to say, at least Rolls's mother had the decency, (if I could call it that) to stay away from her mother and not just hang over her while just waiting for her to die like a vulture, as Terrol did with my Mother.

Another thing I want to add about Roll's case, and he will never admit it because he is not man enough to do so, but he knows I saved his ass from being put in the streets because no other attorney in the City would represent him, and without my calling Beck for him, Mr. Beck would not have taken his case either.

What seems to be the thing to do in the N. E. Portland area, is to Financially Abuse the Elderly because, the property my friend Rolls had to fight to get back was also in the same area just within walking distance away from my Mother's home. But Financial Elderly Abuse is by no means just limited to the State of Oregon or the City of Portland.

While living in Sacramento some 9 years ago I just happened to be at a corner store and as I was headed to my car to leave parked next to me were these 2 ladies sitting in their car. The driver whose name was Linda began a conversation with me asking me if I was at the casino a few nights ago. I told her yes, then she introduced me to her mother who was sitting on the passenger side, her name was Bunny. From that day forward a close friendship evolved and I would take them to the casino sometimes on a regular basis. Linda has a son, his name is John and for some reason he found himself doing time in the State Penitentiary. So over the course of a few years I would take Linda and her mother on a 4 hour round trip to visit that man in prison, they both really loved that man. After several years of being incarcerated John was finally released which pleased those two woman to no end. Things were going well for a few months, the ladies bought him a car, found a nice place for him to live because he couldn't stay with them because they were living in a Seniors only community. Sadly a few months later John totaled out the car, shortly after that he got evicted from his apartment they arranged for him, things were going down hill fast for o'l John. With nowhere to go they were forced to let him stay with them against all the rules risking eviction themselves. So they ended up buying him another car so he could get away from them and spread his wings, of sorts.

Linda is 66 years old and a cancer survivor, her mother Bunny is 86 years old and has physical challenges as well and both are living on limited incomes. Needless to say that John has became an irresponsible burden on these two elderly women, he had no job and soon after they purchased the second car he again got into a accident in that car as well. So in 2017 after a few months of having John staying with them the other seniors in the community began to complain to the association because of the hours John was keeping. Again the women were faced with having to get him some transportation and against their better judgment they ended up renting him a car so he could get out of the house and hopefully find a job and or a girlfriend preferably both. Tensions were running high in the household, so high that I even had to allow him to come and stay with me for a few days. But his roots are in the San Francisco Bay area and he couldn't seem to stay away from there and that was in part the reason he had trouble focusing on the task at hand..

Linda and Bunny have always suspected that John was back to his old ways and using which was more than likely the truth and probably the reason why after he left my house and drove to the Bay in the rental car and shortly after he got it towed for one reason or another.

After the rental car got towed John was right back at the house again with nowhere to go and the tension in the air turn to anger thicker than ever, a recipe for disaster. And the reason for that was because he didn't let his mother know that the car was in towed for a week costing her over $500 and that didn't sit well for the women. It just so happened that a month or so before Bunny had received her portion of an inheritance from the sale of property that her parents left her and her sister which was in the thousands and she kept a large portion of it in hidden in her bedroom, John was not aware of the cash Bunny had received. One day shortly after the heated argument about the rental car John had the nerve to ask that they rent him another one, well that didn't go the way he thought it should, they gave him an emphatic no. The next day Linda had to take her mother to her doctors appointment leaving John in the house all alone.

I just want to say, I truly believe that had John approached his mother and grandmother and asked them to lend him money to get an apartment instead of renting him another car, they would have gladly given it to him because his track record with cars was dismal and having him out of their house was just what the doctor ordered. The thought of having his own apartment never crossed John's mind, I think he was just trying to get back down to the Bay to do whatever it was he did down there. While the women were away that gave him time to rumble through the house looking for valuables so he could get back to the Bay, low and behold that man looked in one of his grandmother's purses and hit the

Jack Pot. What he found was 3 envelopes, each one contained $5000, instead of him going in one and taking out a few hundred or taking a few hundred out of each one, the man took all three envelopes. That man stooped so low as to take all that money from not only the Elderly, but it was also his grandmother and mother. John took that money and they have never seen him or heard from him since and its been close to a year, and the word through the grapevine is that the man is in the Bay walking around the streets flat broke and hungry, another case of Elderly Financial Abuse was committed. Those elderly women had mad love for that man and he betrayed them in the worst way.

A few years after Terrol and Geraldine orchestrated the deception against our Mother she, Geraldine took a trip to Oklahoma City, my home town, for a visit. While she was there she reunited with a childhood friend his name is Alvin Gardner, who she met some 45 years earlier when our Mother sent her to spend the summer there. Sometime during the 45 years since she met Alvin and he had became a Preacher at a small church there. And somehow she charmed him enough that he ended up asking her to marry him, I guess they fell in love. It was either that or he was just as lonely a soul as she was both seeking companionship, in any case, (I'm still praying for him to this day) because she said yes. That woman came back to Portland, packed her bags, moved out of her apartment and went back to Oklahoma City and married that man.

Before she left she had to delegate to her daughter Arleta, (Po Thang) to every month go to my Mother's house, cash her Social Security checks, give my Mother's portion of the loan payments to her brother Terrol so he could maintain the notes each month. And that's exactly what Arleta did, she visited my Mother once a month and that was on check day, like clockwork. She went to the store sometimes for my Mother on that day, other than that, my Mother never seen that grandchild on any other day of the month, and this went on for years. In late 2008 was the year that my Mother's health began to decline and she could no longer get up the flight of stairs to get to her bedroom and bathtub so the doctor ordered her a hospital bed to put in her dinning room until she became strong enough to get up the stairs. Well, that never happened, she failed to regain her strength to walk up the stairs again, so my Mother was confined and remained in the dinning room on that twin size-hospital bed for the rest of her life.

ACT-17

Unauthorized Loans

———~~~———

he records at City Hall show that they, Terrol & Geraldine Johnson set forth a plan to use my Mother, Lucille Johnson, as their own (Cash Cow). They took out that unauthorized loan/bogus sale of her home in the amount of $75,000 in May 2003. Three years later, September, 2006 they borrowed and or refinanced her home, (without her knowledge/ permission) in the amount of $85,622.29 and then again took out another loan and or refinance on the home in 2010 in the amount of $85,000, again (without her knowledge.) And if that wasn't enough, they reached back in and again in February of 2013, borrowing the sum of $125,000, once again (without permission.) If that's not an on going conspiracy, What is?

Sadly, but not surprisingly, helping my Mother get out of that dinning room and upstairs to her bedroom, bathroom, and off of that uncomfortable twin-size hospital bed was not on Terrol's (to do list), with any of the monies from those loans he took out in 2010 and 2013.

It was at that time she really needed health aids and financial assistance because she had been trying to sleep on that hospital bed for the better part of two years in 2010. But his inaction to help my Mother only revealed his callousness and indifference to her suffering and the true extent of his greed and narcissism.

One would think that a caring and loving grandson would have used some of that money he borrowed to get my Mother a lift to get her up and down the stairs to get to the van that took her to dialysis 3 times a week, and get her a lift to get upstairs to her bedroom where she had a double King-size bed to sleep in. And too, get her a walk-in bathtub so she could bathe and treat her chronic arthritis 4 or 5 nights a week, which would have cost him just a fraction of the money that he swindled from my Mother. This would have been a small price to pay to make sure his grandmother would live out her last years in comfort, which is what a normal thinking person would have done. The man was out of his mind with greed.

I can't for the life of me figure out what that man did with most of that money he stole from my Mother, but I can tell you what he did with some of it. Well, one of the first things he did was remodeled the two bedrooms upstairs and turning one of them into his personal walk-in closet while my mother was down stairs sleeping on a hospital bed. He then hired people to come in to remodeled the second bedroom, redoing the floors and painting the room where he took up residence in 2003. He then went on to furnish it off by purchasing a new King-size bedroom set, and then he added a 50 inch flat screen TV, which is fine, except when you take into consideration that the T.V. my Mother was watching downstairs was a 12" antiquated model that was previously on her kitchen counter until the T.V. in the living room played out several weeks earlier.

It wasn't until I drove up to see her that month I just happened to stop by to pick up my eldest son Demetrius before going over to the house. When we walked into the house my Mother was sitting in her lounge chair watching television, or kinda. After greeting her he and I sat on the couch to continue talking to her and as we were sitting there my son asked her, "Grandma, can you see that little T.V.?", she replied in her usual cheerful voice, "Yes, baby, I can see it alright", she was in her 90's, and the T.V. was sitting way across the room, my son then said to her, "Grandma, no you can't!" Then he turned to me as he was standing up walking towards the door and said, "Pops, come on". We got into my car and I took him back to his apartment where he had an extra 32" flat screen that they were not using, we took it over to my Mother and he hooked it up for her.

What Terrol had also done is what really bothered me, back in 2012, and to this day, I'll never understand, he without my Mother in mind, made changes to the upstairs bathroom where the only bath tub was. One would have to ask the question, knowing his grandmother needed a bathroom with a walk-in tub, why wouldn't he make it accessible for her, knowing she was down stairs and there was no shower or tub there? It became apparent to me that he was just fixing the house up for himself in anticipation of my Mother passing away soon. You see, during the time he was doing all of this renovation my Mother was 92 years old and she was taking dialysis treatment 3 times a week, and had been doing so for the better part of 3 years, struggling to get around on a walker, so he just felt her days were numbered. But what he failed to understand was that my Mother had no plans of checking out any time soon! Another thing too was that the fact he had took out loans on her house had yet to come to light at this point. And the significance of that, is that they, Geraldine and her son Terrol were banking on my Mother passing before anyone found out that he took out any loans on her house that way they could say that my Mother gave him the house and she wouldn't be around to dispute it, but they got caught because she lived much longer!

Terrol was driving around town in a big Cadillac but that wasn't enough for him, he decided it was time he just had to have a Classic Car as well so he bought one. The man was on a roll, he had to have and buy things, but my Mother, in his eyes needed nothing, so he bought her nothing but continuing to spend her money. In the year or so following he feels the urge to go on this multi-state tour and finds his way one month to the Final Four event, than The Mardi Gras in Louisiana, and when it hits him, he then decides to attend a The Super Bowl, all on my Mother's dime. He is feeling so good about doing these things he felt the need to post his adventures on line, on My Face, Tweeker, or what ever it is those online surfers call those sites, to show and tell all of their business to the world, a pretty dumb thing to do when you are robbing your grandmother blind. He made it seem as though he was this (Big-Baller).

He made it sound as though he worked all of his life for and bought that prime property on n. e. Skidmore, that he took from my Mother. He even went on a site to discuss with other credible home owners about how the city is treating them unfairly, tax wise or some shit, the balls on that man. He is doing all of this while my Mother slept on that small ass hospital bed right next to a cold ass window, catching colds and pneumonia every few months in her crowed ass dinning room. Each time he comes back off one of his trips to her house he gets to go up the stairs to take a hot bath or shower, and sleep in his nice big King-size bed. I just have a huge problem with that because when I think about how that man could walk in and out of that house knowing and seeing my Mother is stumbling around her home day and night in dire need of help and he does nothing to help her. That irks me so profoundly because there was nothing I could do to help her because the house was in his name and I had no finances to help her, my hands were tied. All I could do was to continue helping her with the house payments each month and the annual taxes on it not knowing it would prove to be all in vain.

ACT-18

Daily Routine

—————

Over the years I would drive up each month to visit my Mother I would always sleep on the couch next to the dinning room where she slept so when she needed something I'd be there for her. Each morning and through the night I would wake up and check on her, more often than not she would already be sitting on the side of the bed when I walk in there, she rarely slept through the night.

I would start the morning by going into the restroom off the kitchen and heat up a face towel for her so she could wash her face. Then I would go into the kitchen, turn on her '12' inch T.V. that she kept on the counter top to watch CBS programs. Then I would fill up the coffee pot to brew her must have Folgers coffee and start preparing breakfast for her. On most days either Donna, Lois, or David would walk in the house while we were in the kitchen. Often the girls would come in before we got to the kitchen and go straight into the dinning room to help her get dressed and then, when need be, help towel bathe her. She would then

89

come into the kitchen to her favorite seat by the window where she sat and enjoyed her meals, gazing through the window at all of her plants and the two Giant Fern trees. On the days she didn't have to do dialysis after breakfast we would retreat to the living room and I would sit her in her lounge chair where she would go on to watch her CBS day-time programs starting with, Let's Make A Deal, The Price Is Right, and ending with The Young And The Restless, a 3 hour routine she enjoyed doing every morning since she retired some 25 years earlier. Another daily activity she enjoyed doing when the weather permitting, and before she was confined to her porch, was to go out to her large yard to water and take care of all of her beautiful plants, flowers and vegetables that she took so much pride in growing. It was my wish that she had a lift or ramp so that she could take it to get to the sidewalk where see could at least water her plants but, the powers that be at that time, (Terrol) didn't share my concerns, he had no problem just watching her confined to the porch.

Now I found myself for the first time in years unable to provide for my Mother, I had no money to get the lifts, both in or outside of the house, nor could I get her the walk-in tub she so badly needed for her to be comfortable in what was suppose to be her glory years. I felt so helpless, yet vengeful towards those that were in control of my Mother's finances and chose to just watch this beautiful, proud woman slowly loose her independence. In my lifetime I've seen the many ways in which people would mistreat their fellow man/woman for various reasons, but I must say in my Mother's case the degree of nefariousness in which these people perpetrated against her supersedes anything I've ever witnessed or thought could be done to a person for the love of money. I can't reveal the thoughts that were going through my mind about the people that were doing this to my Mother.

ACT-19

Her Caring/ Not So Caring Children

—⁓w⁓—

I so enjoyed being there at the house with my Mother as we always done, just talking and watching television. When it came time to shut it down for the night and go to bed, which was usually late night, (she hated that bed,) she would always say to me, "Bernard, I really wish I could get upstairs to my bedroom". Then she would follow with, "Ok baby, I'm going to go lay down now" then she would get up on her walker and go and sit on that little bed, and try to get comfortable enough to go to sleep. But all through the night she would wake up, call my name, I would go in and check on her, she would be sitting on the side of that uncomfortable hospital bed. I would then go in and sit up with her through the night and talk with her, adjust the bed and or pillows until I made her comfortable enough to get back to sleep. I would always massage her feet and knees with a lotion (Ultimate Originals) that I kept her supplied with that I brought from California that she loved. This went on every night and every time I was there visiting her. It broke my heart to watch this strong, beautiful, and proud woman in such a state and not being able to help her, I knew what see needed but I didn't have the means to provide it.

I could only stay with her a week at a time and then I would have to leave because I had 2 teenagers in school and my wife of 27 years at the time, Diane Sentell, whom herself was going through a bout with cancer. Leaving my Mother knowing that she would be going through that same thing night after night with no one there to comfort her just tore me apart. Terrol wouldn't sleep down there on the couch next to her any night of the week and he was there every night. This was because he had a big king-size bed and big screen T.V. upstairs to get to and smoke his weed. She also had 3 granddaughters but they didn't have the time to rotate and stay with her and care for her at least once or twice a week, why? I don't know why they wouldn't have wanted to have spent more time with that Beautiful Wise O'l Woman and that is beyond me. It wasn't as if either of them were married, or had children to take care of or attend to each night which would have prevented them from staying over a night or two out of their boring, selfish lives. Plus they could have learned a lot about and from her and themselves, from where they came from and more because she had a wealth of knowledge and history to share with them, but they missed out on that.

When my week with her was up I would tear up while driving down the highway thinking about my Mother knowing what she would be going through and that she would be alone and without me being there to help her. she was my Girl!

My sister Ma Donna, who my Mother had a special Love for as well and hoped would go on to have a singing career because she had a voice like a song bird, but it just wasn't in the cards. But she did find a good man, he wasn't rich money wise, but he was rich at heart, and Donna, loves him, and he loves her, but Donna, like myself, was not the marrying kind. They are to this day still together, his name is Berry and he is sweet enough for her, but not for my Mother but, over the years grew to love him too, (kinda).

I took comfort in knowing that Donna, Lois, and or David, one of them would come over every morning, Lois and David had night time jobs, but it wasn't the mornings that concerned me, it was the nights. Even with Donna's own physical challenges, she would step up to the plate, get up every morning to take care of our Mother. She would go over and make sure she took her medication, she would cook her breakfast, help dress and towel bathe her every day, and get her ready for dialysis 3 times a week. She needs to be commended for her efforts in taking care of our Mother the best she could, my Mother was very proud of her as well because she gave her less problems than any of her children.

Now Lois on the other hand my sister/brother, along with her life partner, Phyllis would also make sure our Mother would have home cooked meals at least 3 or 4 times a week. Lois learned the art of cooking from our Mother, although she was a late bloomer in the execution of her cooking skills and that was only because she had her people cooking for her, but she got it together and could really do it well. I say sister/ brother because she back in the days when we were growing up she was the one I looked up to. She was the first girl I knew to have her own car, a car that our Mother's brother, Joe Fred, gave her when he left to go to the Arm Forces. Maaaan!, our Mother was not a Happy Camper when he did that! I don't even think she was even 16 years old when she took possession that 55 Ford, 4-speed with the words, So Rare, written on the side of it. She was a thorn in our Mother's ass after she got that car. Lois was also the one that dropped me down the laundry shoot to our basement when we were living on Knott Street in north Portland in the 1950's, she too was the one that made me her own personal Crash-Car Dummy on all of her home made Go-carts that always seem to crash when I was on it, our Mother didn't know if the bitch was trying to kill me or what. She was also the one that showed me how to put fine creases in my Levi jeans in the early 60's, and she had more girlfriends then any of my brothers. Back then she and others of her lifestyle were known as Tom-Boys. I didn't care what they called her because she made it clear and I knew she really unconditionally loved me, and all of her brothers, (Big-Time!) and it goes without saying, she loved our Mother as well, and she was there for our Mother when she really needed her.

As I mentioned, David Earl, would come over in the mornings to make sure that one of the sisters were there and if not he would make sure our Mother would have her coffee and sometimes cook breakfast for her as well. He would also go shopping for her, and he would too take her to her doctors appointments. He was another one of her sons that she was proud of. I recall not long after we moved in the house on Skidmore we attended Highland grade school just two blocks away from the house. David was only in the 4th grade but he began acting out in school and when the report cards came out that first year he brought home all "F"s on his, he had a problem. That didn't sit well with our Mother, to say the least, so she took out that corporate punishment on that ass because she didn't play that "F" game. And after that, he got the message instantly and she never seen another "F" on his report cards and from that time forward. He started turning in better grades on his report card then any of her other children and went on to be top in his classes all the way through Grade and High School. Plus he had the advantage of being her baby boy, so when he would go to her and tell her I did something to him I would get punished. I really had it in for his ass because of that for a long time but we grew out of that and we came to respect each other and became true brothers and I know he loved our Mother as well and he took good care of her.

The year that Terrol put my Mother's house in his name in 2003 and changed the locks on Bernita, she and him became arch enemies for years to come, but Bernita had already became an aversion within the family long before this took place. He could keep her out of the house for the most part but what he couldn't do was keep Bernita out of my Mother's life. After awhile Bernita finagled her way back in the graces of my Mother, (sort of), at least to the point where they were talking again. No one in the family could understand what she had on my Mother or why she wouldn't just completely cut her off. But I could, the reason being is because I knew Bernita, and I must say, had that child used her wits in a positive manner she could have really made something of herself. Its was just simply the way she was wired that seemingly gave her more pleasure in living on the dark side. It was as if the thrill of taking from people, hurting people and getting away with it gave her some sort of sadistic satisfaction. She also had a way with people, my Mother especially that would disarms them allowing her to take total advantage of them. Bernita was truly a piece of work but likeable in a weird way to some people, in and outside of the family. She was even able to ease her way back into Terrol's, and Donna's good grace at times, they never trusted her again but they would talk to her and be somewhat tolerant of her. (Full Disclosure) I even let her back in my life from time to time after a few years because she did make a half ass sincere effort to make amends to my Mother. She would call her on a daily bases she would also pay a bill for her periodically and even take her a few dollars sometimes, but not nearly enough to cover what she owed. She'd come to see her periodically when Terrol was at work to avoid conflict, Plus I didn't hate her, I just hated how she treated my Mother. She never stopped being herself, this was just the way she was wrapped and it worked for her. She was also able to get away with it for many years without getting prosecuted for her actions or get killed by someone, she was indeed a miserable soul.

In August 2013 as I was leaving Portland driving down Interstate-5 on my way back to Sacramento and it just occurred to me that its been 10 years since Terrol put my Mother's house in his name. My Mother had been confined to that dinning room for the better part of 5 years, and after several attempts over five years without success to convince Terrol to add my Mother back on title, this could be the time. So I pulled off at the next rest stop and called Bernita because I knew if anybody could do it, she would be the one to find out about the status of the house, so I instructed her to run a make on the house. She called me back a day or two later with what she had uncovered and it was the document that showed the transfer of my Mother's property to Terrol which seemed to indicate that she had sold her home to him for $75,000. While I was trying to process the reality of what that woman just informed me of, it became clear to me as to why that man didn't want to talk to me when I approached him over all those years to put my Mother back on title and why he refused to do so. That bit of information gave credence to what my uncle J.D. was suspicious of all along, because my uncle did approach me some years earlier and he too told me to keep an eye out on Geraldine and Terrol.

After getting that information from Bernita I again told Terrol to put her back on title and again he refused, so finally I said to him " Mother Fucker, why won't you put her back on title, my Mother needs help!" and I used that language to him because, I felt he was indeed trying to Fuck my Mother out of her house, and I was right. And his response was, "if I put her on title and she gets the lift and tub the State would put a lien on the house and would want their money back when she died," I said "WHAT?, So Fuck'en What? This is her house, my Mother worked all of her adult life for this house and that is exactly why she did, so that she could have security when she needed it!"

He then said to me, "I told you my position on this matter" and hung the phone up on me. I have to say, it took every fiber in my being not to jump in my car and drive up there with my pistol and shoot that man in his knee cap about his position on my Mother's life! With the stroke of a pin my Mother could have had the things she needed to live the rest of her life comfortably, the life she worked so hard for and deserved to have. And now this Nigga had the power to help her in his hands and refused to do so because of money and property that he didn't even work for and wasn't even his! The ironic thing about his position is that he never once said to me or anyone, "my Grandmother gave me this house", or "I bought this house from my Grandmother, so its mine!" Why? Because he knew it really wasn't his, he was just taking it, and I had he evidence in my hands.

After a couple of days of thinking about just how I was going to deal with this Nigga, I decided to wait for a few more days until I could verify what Bernita had had told me. Now here I'm faced with having to inform my Mother that she had yet again been deceived by another one of her daughters and one of her grandsons. I was reluctant to tell her because of her health issues at that time. She was so looking forward to having her home put back in her name once the loan was paid off which she thought was in the not so distant future. And it wasn't just so much for her to get the medical needs she required, as it was that she just also wanted to live long enough to have her house back in her possession because it was hers and it was important to her to leave it to the family. Knowing this I didn't want send her into a depression by revealing to her the magnitude of the betrayal, she was 93 years old and I knew this was something she really wasn't ready to hear at that stage of her life.

Over the next couple of days I'm thinking how could I let her know that she would now have to fight in the courts to get her home back from Geraldine and Terrol. This was something I couldn't discuss with her over the phone and I was due to drive up there in a couple of weeks but I decided to drive back up there a few days later. I decided to wait to confront Terrol as well, I wanted to ask him about the $75,000 loan/sale he took out on the house in 2003 and why. When Terrol took out that loan my Mother's health was pretty well intact and she was still able to get up and down the stairs, get to her bedroom and get in the tub with little or no help even though she was 83 years old. But I still have a problem with the fact that they didn't respect her enough to let her know about the $50,000 loan and didn't even give her any of it.

That circumstance was the beginning of the financial abuse and conspiracy that continued through the 10 years. What truly pisses me off about this criminal activity perpetrated against my Mother is that after several years when she no longer could do for herself it didn't even bother Terrol to watch her struggling to walk around that house with the help of a walker due to her chronic arthritis. He also watched her being put in a wheel chair 3 days a week to go to her dialysis treatments having to be carried down the front stairs by the workers that was sent to take her for years. While all the time he was robbing her with these loans he was taking out how cold and calculating is that, and what kind of person does that to anybody, let alone to their own Grandmother?

My Mother was a Strong and Proud Woman, and unfortunately for them, another five years had passed, now its 2013 and she is still here and the full scope of the Financial Abuse that they had perpetrated against my Mother came to light that year. They never expected my Mother to live pass 90. You see, although my Mother had physical challenges, her mind was as strong as a steal trap and she loved life and all of her children and she fought off the Grim Reaper for a long time, for that reason, although a few of them didn't deserve her true love. My Mother was a fighter and soldier in her own right, as was her son Louis, he got it honestly from her. I'm angry with myself because I couldn't raise enough finances needed to get my Mother her life prolonging amenities, I feel as if I let her down because she counted on me to look after her and protect her from those Parasites that were bleeding her dry. Back in January of 2013 my brother David and I went so far as to call in a contractor over to get an estimate on what it would cost to expand the restroom off the kitchen (which was difficult for her to navigate to because she was on a walker), to add a walk-in tub. The quote he gave us was north of $20,000 and because the house was not in her name he required half the money down and a respectable credit score, neither of which any of us had.

On my drive to Portland that following week I was trying to figure out how I was going to tell my Mother that her daughter and grandson had took her home, I was not looking forward to that conversation. When I arrived to the house she was at her dialysis treatment so I knew I couldn't break the news to her on that day because those are the days she is at her weakest. So I just made sure she had something to eat when she came home. As I was in the kitchen preparing my Mother's meal Terrol walked in the house, it was just he and I. I know he noticed my car sitting in my Mother's Disable parking space in front of the house when coming up the stairs but he didn't bother to speak when he came in, he just went straight up stairs to his room. I just went in the living room and sat there until he came back down I then called him in so I could get some answers. I thought being as though I was armed with this incriminating document from the Hall Of Records that I had some leverage to get him to put my Mother back on title. When he came down the stairs to leave, I called him in the livingroom and asked him did he let my Mother know that he borrowed that extra $45-50,000 in 2003, he told me no, I asked him why, he had no answer. That statement/ non-statement from him confirmed what I suspected from the start and that was my Mother never knew what she was signing that day in 2003, if she was the one that signed it at all. I said to him, "Ok Tee, look man, all of that is in the past, just put my Mother's name back on title so she can get the tub and lift and we will worry about telling Mother about that extra money you borrowed later."

What that man said to me in response rose above astonishment, he said, "The reason I won't put her back on title too is because I don't want to have to deal with her children and all they are doing anyway is just waiting around for her to die" unquote. The man was talking to me as if he didn't think I was one of her children, thus, not including me as one of her children waiting for my Mother to die. For him to think that it was alright for him to say such a thing to me about them, was in that moment in time clarification to me that he had been (Touched) by Satin himself. He would rather see my Mother suffer then to have a court battle with my siblings over what was their birth right, he wanted it all! Had he limited his wild accusations to just Bernita he might have gotten a more sympathetic ear, maybe, because what he said was even a stretch for her because although she was off her rocker, I know she didn't wish for my Mother to die. For that man to make such a blanketed statement about my siblings was unacceptable on so many levels and could not have been further from the truth it just let me know that he let greed put him on the verge of loosing his mind. The ironic thing about his reckless accusations towards my siblings is that one could argue, and quite convincingly I might add, is that it was he and his mother that were the ones that were more likely being the ones that would be awaiting my Mother's death. After all it was only those 2 that would benefit from her passing. His statement put me in the mind of a cheating husband/wife accusing the other of cheating to mask their own infidelity.

Once I readjusted my jaw after picking it up off the floor in response to what Terrol just said to me, I just told him, "no matter what your issues are with my siblings my Mother needs a tub and lift in this house, and she needs it now!. So what are you going to do about it?" He then replied to me, "I guess i will try and get a loan". As he got up to walk out I stopped him and said to him " Terrol, I love you man but from what you just said to me I gather you are trying to take my Mother's house. It seems too you have intentions on taking my siblings inheritance as well, well, that is between you and them. I don't give a damn about this house or my inheritance, but I'm not going to just sit back and let you take it, but first and foremost I want you to do the right thing for my Mother and you need to do it now!".

What he said in response to that was," B, (that's what he calls me) man I've been paying on this house for ten years" I then said to him, " my Mother and I have been paying on this house as well, for that same ten years, and of course you been paying on it for ten years because you took out an unauthorized loan on this house and that just means you own the debt, not this house!" He then just nodded his head in the affirmative as he walked out on me. Mind you, I still don't know about the other loans this man took out on her home at this point.

I decided to wait to tell my Mother about what was going on with him, and her daughter about her house. This was not easy for me because I knew this news would break her down, I was just waiting for the right time. I was in hope that he would go ahead and do the right thing and add her back on soon now that we had that little face-to-face. I thought I'd give him a few days to make the necessary moves to put her back on title.

To my surprise Bernita kept her word and she said nothing to our Mother about what Terrol and Geraldine had done to her. But she had to tell somebody so she chose to tell our brother David, and why did she do that? It just so happened that David had a friend in the real estate business, the same agent that sold him his house. He called her and had her run a complete make on Mother's property, a couple of days later she got back to him with her findings and it wasn't pretty. It turned out that Bernita had only discovered a portion of the deceitful actions that had been perpetrated against our Mother. David called me on the day I was planning to leave and asked me meet him at the land mark (Over Look Restaurant/Bar) just down the street from the house to have lunch and because he had something he wanted to show me.

Once I arrived and walked into on the restaurant side I didn't see him so I went over to the Bar side where I saw him sitting at the bar. I walked up to the bar where he sat and ordered a Bud light, it was about high noon. I glanced over to see what he was drinking and I noticed he had in his hand a snifter filled with Brandy, I said, "hey Bro, ain't it a bit early to be drinking that stuff?", he replied, "you will want to trade that Bud in for a double shot of Remy Martin after I show you these papers", while sliding me this plastic folder. The folder contained documents dating back to the year when our Mother purchased her home and all other transactions pertaining to that house up until 2013. The most interesting documents were the ones that showed loans taken out on the house by Terrol and there were three more then Brenita found. The man not only took out that loan/bogus sale in 2003, but he also took out one in 2006, 2010, and another one in February of 2013. After going over those documents I became overwhelmed with a series of emotions which were rolling around in my mind like a Roulette Wheel not knowing which or where that little white ball would land. Those Parasites has successfully and systematically drained nearly half of my Mother's equity out of her home without her knowledge and did nothing to help that Beautiful O'l Woman, who were these people? I turned to David and said, "I'm ready for that double shot of Remy now!" He looked at me with fire in his eyes and said, " What are we going to do about this Big-Bro?, I know what I want to do" I replied, "I know what I want to do as well D, but we can't." So after he and I sat there drinking for a while just thinking about how we were both so negligent in allowing this to happen and what we both wanted to do to him for doing it, cooler heads prevailed. We then just ordered some dinner for Mother so she could have something to eat when she came home from dialysis that evening and we went our separate ways.

Ok now it was clear that the week time line I gave Terrol to put our Mother back on title was null and void, so I had to just gather the strength to go and let our Mother know what her beloved First-Lady daughter and grandson had done to her. We couldn't do it that day because it was dialysis day and she would be too weak to hear such devastating news so I decided to waited until the next day. When morning came as I'm preparing breakfast for her all the while dreading the moment when I would have ruin a perfectly beautiful morning by telling her that she was once again betrayed so badly this time by another one of her other daughters. After breakfast we went into the living room to watch her daytime programs as usual and as we were doing so I turn the volume down and said to her, " Mother, I have to tell you something" she said, "What is it Bernard?" I proceeded to show her the papers in folder that David gave me while explaining what they meant, I told her, 'This is proof that your first-lady daughter, Geraldine and your grandson Terrol are in the process of taking your house and that they have already robbed you for more than $100,000 in loans on your house". As I was finishing explaining to her what happened, in walked Donna and she saw the tears in our Mother's eyes. She said, "Mama, whats wrong?" she replied, " Bernard just told me that Geraldine and Terrol took my house from me, I can't believe Geraldine would let Terrol do that to me" and she just broke down.

Seeing my Mother weeping like that pierced my heart once again, the last time I saw her in such pain is when I came back from Denver in 2008 after attending my brother Louis's funeral.

Donna, when she saw Mother crying and realized just how hurt she was about the situation she was livid and she too began crying. And Donna has a mild and passive demeanor, but a real Diva in her own right and there was not much that could ever upset her except what Bernita did to her and our Mother, and now seeing what those other two parasites had done to Mother, I was now standing there having to try and calm them both down.

So what I end up doing was contacting my attorney, Beck, and put him on the case because it was clear that the fix was in and Terrol or his mother Geraldine had no intention on putting the house back in my Mother's name. It was only by the Grace of her God that he kept her here long enough so that she could learn and see what Judases were living in her mist. It was as if he, her God, wanted her to know this before he called her to come live with him in his House, because that's exactly where that Beautiful Woman is today.

That boy, not man, walk around there all of those years and in February of 2013 seeing my Mother needing help in every way, more than ever, and the court documents show, that he just borrowed/refinanced that house for $125,000 which netted him at least $40,000 that he could have helped her with in that year and still didn't help my Mother, If that wasn't an on going conspiracy of Financial Elderly Abuse Case, there is no such thing.

What they didn't factor in was that my Mother was not ready to leave this earth on his time table. This so called man, and his so called first lady mother, allowed and watched my Mother struggle around (Her Home), on a walker and in pain, and suffering. She could barely get into that tiny ass restroom near the kitchen, where there was only a toilet and sink, never being able to take a bath for years. They could have made it possible for her to have a walk-in tub so she could bathe herself and keep some semblance of dignity in her last years of her life. What kind of persons would not be on board to do that?!

That was like watching someone die a slow death and being able to help them, and not doing anything about it, and it was all about greed and profit for them. They already had the house, how could you watch your Grandmother suffer like that?! Why didn't his mother, Geraldine, demand that her son used that money he borrowed in 2013 to help her own mother?

Before I hired my lawyer to take her case, my sister Geraldine would call my Mother every day, many times two or three times a day, and she did that for years. Once she found out that my Mother was seeking to get her name back on title so she could get the lifts and walk-in tub she needed, Geraldine stopped the phone calls for months. When she did finally call her again she didn't say, "Mother, why are you attempting to put your name back on title? You know you sold that house to my son Terrol, and he paid you!" Well, I'll tell you why she didn't say it, she didn't say it because it never Happened! If that wasn't enough, Terrol, is this man that stands 6'2, 260 lbs., when he learned that my brother David took our Mother to talk to my attorney and was subsequently served and put on notice, he came storming down the stairs and stood towering over this Beautiful frail woman while she was sitting in her lounge chair, watching television and at the top of his voice said to her, "How can you be suing me to get you're your name back on title after all I've done for you?" then he stormed out of the house, slamming the door on that Beautiful O'l helpless woman! My question to that is, "why didn't he just calmly walk down the stairs and say to her, (Gradma, you sold me this house, don't you remember?) The answer to that question too, is simple, because it never happed! What kind of person would storm down stairs and confront their 93 year old grandmother in such a fashion? I submit to you, only a deranged person with a death wish would commit such an act because no sane person would disrespect a Matriarch in that fashion knowing the consequences he could face would result in him being permanently disabled and or his premature demise, trust me, he was really pressing his luck! All that boy did for my Mother was rob her blind and disrespect her!

After he verbally abused my Mother she call me crying and terrified at the way in which he talked to her, and she was in fear now that the man was going to now put her out of her own house. It wasn't enough that they were conspiring to take her money and house, now they had this Beautiful O'l woman living in fear in her own home! So you know now I really wanted to drive up there and shoot this Nigga in his ass and or in both knees now!

What is not so surprising to me about these low-life criminals is that they have just been very lucky because there are a lot of criminals that are incarcerated for far less.. Anyone can commit a crime, but, getting away with it is and should be, and is suppose to be the objective. The plan they had to take my Mother's home looked good on paper and it would have worked, their only problem was that, they didn't factor in the fact of my Mother's will to live, and that she would live to be 94 years old and being with sound of mind. The Real Crime here is that they did nothing to help my Mother to reach that Milestone, it was all her! Had they helped her, she would very well still be here!

You see, its not so much as what a criminal says that is telling, but what they don't or can't say that is even more revealing and will get them caught and busted every time. These two brilliant criminal minds together chose to, intimidate, slam doors on her, and even give her the silent treatment, but neither of them together couldn't find the courage to face this Beautiful 93/94 year O'l woman on a face-to-face basis and tell her, Mother/Grandmother, you sold your home to Terrol for $75,000! There is something (Truly) wrong with that picture.

ACT-20

The Investigation

———〜〜〜———

$\mathcal{A}$nother thing these thieves didn't know is that the Adult Protective Service Investigator in Portland Oregon got involved and came to my Mother's home and talked to my Mother and sister Donna about the financial abuse. Mr. Don Cheperka of Adult Protective Service was told by my Mother that she knew nothing about and had not authorized any of the loans that Terrol had taken out on her home, and that's on the record. He, Mr. Cheperka made a couple attempts to visit and contact Terrol at the house on this matter but was unsuccessful.

But after Mr. Cheperka did his investigation and he determined that there was probable cause to go forward with this case to the next level and he turned his findings over to the criminal division. What was unfortunate for my Mother's case was that the detective that Mr. Cheperka turned the case over to was a detective by the name of Uttkey. It turns out that Detective Uttkey was either, a rooky, incompetent, bias, or any combination of the above.

In November of 2013 an article posted on Oregonian/Oregon Live, by Brent Hunsberger, focuses on the increase of Financial Abuse against the Elderly in Oregon, he went on to say, "The number of financial abuses alleged by the elderly and disabled in Oregon increased 33 percent between 2009 and 2012 to 2,870, says the state." "According to the state of Oregon, family members are accountable for more than half of all alleged financial abusers, with (Daughters) being the most frequent perpetrators. In 37 percent of substantiated thefts involving money, the perpetrators had legal powers over the victim's finances."

This article mirrors just what my Mother was going through, she was helpless against those greedy street wise criminals with her daughter Geraldine at the helm.

Obviously Detective Uttkey failed to do her home work or didn't get that memo, because the only investigating she did was look at the suspicious document dated in 2003 that stated, and showed that $75,000 was conveyed to my Mother, from Terrol. That coupled with a phone conversation my Mother had with the state when she was applying for medical assistance where they asked my sister if my Mother owned property. During that phone call my sister, Geraldine or Donna told them no, she said no because the house was no longer in her name, and those two findings was the extent of Uttkey's investigation. She, the detective was provided with phone numbers to my two sisters and my brother so she could contact them, she never called any of them! She was also provided with my Mother's number plus her attorney's number, Lawrence J. Beck, who just happens to be one of the top lawyers on the West Coast, if not in the country, she never called either of them. What was so ironic about her investigation/non-investigation, is that she never even interviewed my Mother, or her brother J.D, or any contacts that was provided to her, not even Terrol himself.

110

Had she talked to Terrol she would have ascertained that he never said that he gave my Mother any parts of that $75,000 for her home, that was never even his defense to the lawsuit. The detective was told that, but she just ignored that fact. She had a Slam-Dunk case against him, had she only talked to anybody.

My Mother's case should be classified on the records in Portland as a Miscarriage of Justice, because had she not died on September 27th 2014, she would have won her civil case and her home would have been returned to her and I believe that she would have had a few more years left on this earth. Lucille Johnson was not only abused financially but mentally, and emotionally as well by the people she most trusted. Had the detective investigated this case properly my Mother could have gotten the justice she so deserved. All the pain and suffering she went through because of those greedy and insensitive parasites, contributed to her premature death. Because they deliberately ignored my Mother's condition, seeing it in decline everyday, and did nothing to help her, it could be argued that their actions were tantamount to a voluntary or involuntary man slaughter charge, and they should be charged as such. I know that there are a lot of criminals in Portland that are praying that this Detective Uttkey chick is the one that is assigned to their cases.

There are a lot of things about this case that are disturbing but one in particular shows how greed can take preference over compassion. How my Mother's (so called) Christian First Lady daughter, Geraldine and her Military grandson, Terrol could take the position that it was alright for my Mother to be barely walking around that house with the help of a walker and having to take towel baths for the last years of her life when they had the means to help her. My Mother lived 18 months after the date Terrol borrowed $40,000 without sitting in a bathtub in her own home. Everyone knows that hot baths sooths the pain of arthritis and that a woman needs to bathe on a daily basis for hygiene purposes, they didn't even care about that, all they care about was her money and her house.

Had it not been for my brother David, my sisters, Lois, and Ma'Donna, my Mother would have been at the non-mercy of Gerladine and her children, Arleta, and particularly Terrol, and as they hoped, she would have died years earlier before the truth came out. I would hope, for her husband's sake that Geraldine gets her big ass in bathtub at least once a week, because she didn't care if my Mother did! No person in their right mind would think that what those people did to my Mother was acceptable, and anyone that does, there is something really wrong with them too!.

I can't see how Geraldine can even walk inside any church without her wig/weave catching on fire, or how Terrol could walk around my Mother's house, after she died, without having the floors or the ceilings caving in on him, because of the Luciferian tactics they chose to impose on my Mother, those people are sick with greed. What really pisses me the Fuck off about what they did is that that man couldn't find the money to make changes to my Mother's house to accommodate her while she was alive, but just a few months after she died, he finds the money to do a full restoration on the house once again to benefit him and his mother! And the Truth be known, if it weren't for my wife of over a quarter century and my beautiful children, I would probably be writing this biography from a state penitentiary somewhere.

ACT-21

Forgiveness

—⟋⟋⟋⟋—

My Mother passed away in 2014 and I still feel the pain of her absents to this day four years after the fact. I talked to several people about what these Parasites did to her, and over a couple of years I visited a few churches and talked to preachers, but I never did hear from my brother-in-law preacher Alvin after my Mother's funeral. I talked to what few friends I have left, I even talked to people I didn't even know. I also talked to my eldest daughter, who is herself a very religious soul, and in all cases the people would end up telling me, (Bernard, you have to forgive them.) (You have to forgive them in order for you to move on.) I even group text a few people a couple of years ago about how I felt about how they violated my Mother. I received a text back from this one Mental Case Bitch and she had the nerve to text me back and say, "Bernard, you need to get over that Old shit and move on". I promptly replied, "What?!, Bitch, I don't know what planet you are from but on this one 18 months is not old in the grieving process and for the people that abused my Mother, that will never get old. I already knew you were a Mental case and that insensitive and retarded statement just confirmed it. And the only thing that is Older and Drier on this planet is You! (DeeDee!)".

Another one of the people that was a part of that group text was my niece, Rolanda, and she just happens to be one of Terrol's biggest fans. She too felt that I should forgive him and his mother saying that " My father was angry at my half sister for swindling our other grandmother out of all the equity of her home some years earlier and when he decided to forgive her he felt so much better and that he made piece with his daughter, thus giving himself piece with what she did to his mother" I said, "Well, he's a bigger man than me! Plus, he forgave his daughter, not his sister or nephew".

Rolonda is one of the granddaughters I mentioned earlier that lives only 5 minutes away from my Mother house and didn't have time to ever go over to spend a night or two a week with her grandmother all the years she was ill and couldn't do for herself.

Wow! Did you just read what I just wrote in that last paragraph? It just dawned on me! What I just wrote means that Rolonda's sister Fucked their father out of his inheritance and then some years later her favorite cousin Terrol, Fucked her mother, my sister, Rosizean out of her inheritance as well. And her mother, unlike her father, really needed her's, and even to this day still needs its more than ever because she is sitting in a convalescent home and has been there for the better part of three years and will probably end up dying there. If she had the money Terrol fucked her out of, she could be home with her grandchildren. Terrol don't give a shit about my sister, yet Terrol is still Rolonda's favorite person, go figure. There was a time when I was having lots of money she considered me to be her favorite person. Over the years when I was residing in Hawaii I use to pay her to run errands for me one of which was to go to down town Portland and pick up my suit coats from my tailor, Al Lenzer, and she would send them to me there, I even bought my favorite niece a car. I guess now that Terrol has claimed sole ownership of the family home and driving around in Cadillac's, Continentals, and Classic cars off the ill gotten gains from my Mother and the fact that, according to her, I owe her a few hundred of dollars, she demoted me from her favorite persons list. Aside from that it is just hard for me to comprehend how a person could be a friend to someone who has so blatantly mentally, physically, and financially abuse their mother/grandmother, I just don't get it!

She and all in the family knew how much I loved and cared for my Mother and how I did the same for her mother, Rosizean as well. I sent for her mother and financed her relocation to Denver in the early 1980's so that she could better her life and that is where she remains to this day. Anyone who could befriend and defend persons like Terrol and or his mother knowing what they did to my Mother, well, I'm sorry but I have a bitter taste in my mouth and feel some kind way about them because the actions those two took against my Mother were wrong on so many levels. This man Terrol, that became angry at me for calling his mother a bitch, well, I must ask him, "How angry should I be at you for standing by watching my Mother barely getting around her house, while you were robbing her, and not helping her?" To put the two offenses in perspective, (me calling his mother a Bitch) is like comparing the size of a house fly) to (him robbing and watching my Mother die and doing nothing to help her) to a California Condor, are you serious man?!

But wait, it gets even better than that, you can't make this kind of shit up, it occurred to me over the years that perhaps Terrol might had gotten his inspiration to violate my Mother from what his cousin did to her grandmother because she was never held accountable for violating that old woman.

115

Earlier too, he was old enough at the time to understand that his uncle Roy, my brother, swindle me out of one of my homes and he too got away with it. He got away with it only because I gave him a pass, he was my Mother's first child and she was still alive at that time. And although I had the wherewithal to reek havoc on him and his life, I considered my Mother's feelings and I just gave him that pass.

What is wrong with these people these days that they feel entitled and think they can just take property and money from anyone especially their Elders without consequence? I can't answer that question, but what I do know for sure is that those that do it are all very lucky, as was my brother, because there are many people in this country that would not be so understanding or so forgiving to a person that would have the nerve to take from them what is rightfully theirs.

Case in point, I had a friend, his name was, Big Al, we gambled and partied together from time to time through the years. He had this nice and beautiful woman and they had been together for more than 15 years. Her mother and or father passed away years ago and left her and her brother a large sum of money. The check came to her, she for some reason felt entitled to all of the money and told him as much. That man caught a flight from Atlanta Georgia to the west coast and tracked her down in San Francisco California and asked her again for his portion of his money and again she refused to give it to him. That man left that house and came back a day or two later, knocked on her door and when she answered he shot her in the head killing her, then went into the house, shot and killed my friend too, all about his inheritance. So I say again that the parasites that did my Mother are very lucky in that it is just not in my DNA that I would take such measures of going around killing people over money.

But I must say, the shooter did his deed over money, my situation was about my Mother's health and longevity, but I would be lying if

I said that it didn't cross my mind on a few occasions to go off on the deep end about her. Because, the shooter too, who I didn't know, was, as I am, from the Old School, where there are codes and unwritten laws we lived by and the top three of them are as follows: First, you don't mess with a man's/woman's mother, Second, you don't mess with a man's wife, and Third, you definitely don't mess with a man's/ woman's money!

Terrol and Geraldine were in violation of two of them, which meant they put themselves in danger of street justice. When it comes to money, there is an Old saying in the streets, "A Baby can have it, but, a Guerilla can't take it!" Now, what that shooter did and what others like him have done for a lot less, I personally don't condone but, I do understand why they do it!

ACT-22

The Grieving Process

As I mentioned, my Wife of 30 years, Diane passed away close to 18 months after my Mother and she too was a Christian and God fearing woman, she too told me I needed to forgive them, and she loved my Mother deeply. But it wasn't until after she passed that I even considered forgiving them. After she passed I was then grieving two of the most significant Women of my life in as many years and those were the most trying days of my life as well.

When my wife passed I never received a text, a card, nor a phone call of condolences from Terrol, his sister, or his mother Geraldine, nor from her preacher husband, which only let me know that those people hated me for trying to protect and prolong my Mother's life, oh well, I can live with that. So several months after Diane's passing I had to draw all the strength I had left in me to text some of those same people I text before and let them all know I had come to a place where I could finally say I forgive those that trespassed against my Mother. Once I did that I got a flurry of text messages praising me for taking that step to forgive those parasites.

People were saying to me, (that's a good thing Bernard, you are now going to start feeling better), (that's good Bernard, now you can start moving on and put this passed you), (that's good Bernard, you are going to now be blessed), (God is going to bless you Bernard), shit like that. So as time went on I'm still grieving both, my Mother and my Wife Big-Time.

All I have left of them are a few photos of them both in my home, and of course my beautiful daughters, Da'Narsha and Jenaiah that Diane had for me. I find myself talking to both of them, my Mother and Diane, photo wise, and as strange as it may seem to some people it became the norm for me for a while, I miss them both so much!

It finally got to the point where I just couldn't take it anymore. First of all, the only reason I even considered forgiving them was because I was Double Grieving and it was weighing too heavy on my heart and mind, I thought by me forgiving them, that would relieve me of some of the pain I was feeling, or so I was told by these experts on grieving.

Don't misunderstand me, I truly appreciated what the some of those people were trying to do for me, but the fact of the matter is that, there is no (one-size fits all or cookie cutter solution) when it comes to grieving. After a year of my wife passing, it was only 60 days earlier that my Mother's birthday came around. And I'm not feeling any better, in fact, I'm feeling worse, so I'm wondering what happened to: ("Oh Bernard, you are going to feel better when you forgive them"?) I'm looking at my Mother's photos, there are a few of them, one family photo where you can see the pride she has on her face, all of her off springs are in the same room with her, and then there are a couple that were taken after she found out that her daughters and grandson had betrayed her and you can see the sadness and disappointment in the expression on her face. This is what prevents me from moving on and getting passed what they took her through and took from her. I just can't wrap, the thought of anyone that would cause pain to my Mother in any way, and to conspire to harm her in such away, around my head, and that just magnifies the contempt I have for those degenerates that did it to her!

How I'm I supposed to forgive someone that could walk around my Mother everyday, for years just waiting and just watching her, knowing she needs help in every way and not do anything to help her, well, I'm sorry, I tried, but I have to say simply, I have a Huge problem with that and its not going away anytime soon, if ever!

My Mother would have taken a bullet for me! I'm not going to diminish her Glorious and Courageous time on this earth by siding with the masses in their thinking, that by forgiving those for the wrong they did to my Mother will somehow make me feel better and God will Bless me. That may apply to the average crime, but, the treatment and crimes committed against my Mother was so over the top, anything short of prosecution will not suffice.

When it comes to how those Parasites violated my Mother, and it came to forgiving them for it, in anticipation or hoping God is going to Bless me for doing so, there is no contest, I'll never forgive them! And I'll tell you why.

First of all, God has already Blessed me in so many ways, I was Blessed being born to a Mother like Lucille Johnson, God has blessed me by allowing me to be on this earth long enough to see 5 of my 6 children grow to adulthood and become decent and productive citizens, Second, I was shot in the neck with a 38 caliber bullet in 1970,and by the Blessing of God I'm still here, Third, and more over God, blessed me to have had in my life five of his most Beautiful Female creations and all of them truly loved me, and all of them stayed with me for years, most men are lucky to have one. All of them knew and loved my Mother as well, and she knew and loved all of them.

Frankly speaking, I know it is said that God makes no mistakes, but I can argue that there are a number of Bernard Johnsons in this country alone and just maybe one of God's (Guardian Angle's/Secretaries) may have misfiled and gave me a few blessings that belonged to one of them because I've had so many Blessing from him I'm even amazed.

In any case, I'm not going to Dis-Honor my Mother by forgiving those Judases that stood by and watched her die a slow death because they wanted her money and her house, on the off chance or even if the odds were in my favor a Zillion to 1 that I would receive another blessing from God, would I even take that bet. I wouldn't sell my Mother out like that, I don't need or expect any more blessing, I've lived a rich, beautiful, and blessed life. I'll never forgive them!

And I want to state something just for record, and that is, my anger and distain for Terrol and his mother Geraldine has nothing to do with the house or the money they stole from my Mother, as Geraldine would suggest, it all has to do with the mistreatment and betrayal my Mother. You see as far as money goes, for well over twenty 25 years of my life, unlike those bottom feeders, that violated my Mother, (who never owned anything in their lives until they stole from my Mother) God blessed me in that area too, and I've touched and spent hundreds of thousands of dollars on an annual basis in years past.

I've traveled across this country from Los Angeles to New York and other parts of the world, I've met some very influential and not so influential people during those travels. I won't drop names because that is not necessarily a blessing to have done so, but it was interesting. I've met and blessed some of the most poorest people in few of the countries I lived and visited. I've lived a blessed life, I've owned homes, drove Cadillac's off of showroom floors, and I flown first class anywhere I wanted to. There was a time I had and maintained a 6 figure Swiss bank account for years, I've even rubbed shoulders and entertained Royalty.

At one time in my life I possessed a wardrobe that even impressed a Royal Prince from the oil rich nation of Kuwait, his name was Prince Kha'Lid, he was a tennis partner of mine. He excepted a dinner invitation at my home in Denver where we talked business one evening. As I was giving him a tour of the house he walked into one of my bedrooms, which I actually converted into a closet, and when he laid eyes on what was in it, which was a room full of tailor made suits, cut by two of the most prolific tailors in the country (Al Lenzer) of Portland, and (Itzu Sumii) of Las Vegas (may they both rest in peace, man, do I miss them!) (Google them).

That young Prince, Ka'Lid turned to me and said in amazement, ("Bernard, I know Sheiks, and your wardrobe is just as impressive!"). There were so many beautiful handmade, made to order, reptile shoes in that room that one of the largest Cobblers in Tokyo, (Calzeria HOSONO) made for me, I haven't had to buy a pair of dress shoes in over 30 years. Prince Kha'Lid and I were about the same size and he couldn't help himself, he asked me if he could try on a few of the suit jackets, before we sat down to dine and talk, how could I say no to a Prince? He and I had plans to go into business together but unfortunately for me and even more unfortunately for him in 1990 Saddam Hussein invaded his country and he had to fly back to check on his family and I never heard from him again. I'm saying all this to let people know, I've already lived and been Blessed by God in life and I could cite at least a half dozen more examples of blessings God has bestowed upon me but I won't because this is not about me.

This is about my Mother and how they disrespected and mistreated her, her well being was my concern, not the little money she may or may not have left me. There is only one thing that is worst then watching a loved one, especially your mother, struggling to hang on to life knowing that if you had money you could help them, which was the case with my Mother, they could have helped her because they had her money and they chose not to help her, that was my issue!

Again, as was mentioned earlier, Terrol and I were a team and as far as him having that house would not have been an issue to me, had he not violated my Mother. I could have gotten any amount of money I wanted from him, that's how close we were, and we could have still remained friends if he would have just taken care of my Mother! I could have worked out something with him and we could worked out something that would have satisfied my brother and sisters so they could get at least some parts of their birth-right inheritance and we all could have had access to the family home as to our Mother's wishes. And I just want to put this out there too, despite want Geraldine said about why I was upset about Terrol having my Mother's home which was that (I was broke and needed money) which was not the case. Although I retired from the life in 1995 and settled down to raise my daughter and sons, little did she or anybody know is that I had prepared myself financially and I have been living a very comfortable life even to this day.

I've learned how to live without all the jewels, new cars, and going to the tailors every month, I'm passed all that, its been all about raising, educating my children and seeing about my Mother. If it was about money with me, I could have very easily sided with Terrol and his mother to go against my other siblings to take the house as Geraldine did, and they would have loved for me to have been on their team, but thats not who I am, because I love all of them especially our Mother. And when they fucked over my Mother and just watch her die like that, all bets were off! There is not that much money or forgiveness in the world!

ACT-23

Apology?

———〰———

When I drove up to Portland in February of 2014 my Mother and I were talking and she told me that Terrol came down the stairs in a weak attempt to apologize to her for what he had done to her over the years. She said that it was the first time he talked to her since she hired Mr. Beck. and he slammed the door on her. I then said to her, "Well Mother, the damage has already been done, he has done nothing there after to try and remedy your situation, did he offer to add you back on the title, offer to get you a lift to get you upstairs to your bedroom and off this hospital bed?, did he offer to get you a walk-in tub so you could bathe?, did he offer to give you any of your money back!'"? She said "Bernard, the only thing I understood was that he said he borrowed money off the house to pay off some debts, he was sorry for slamming the door on me, the rest of what he said was too slurred because he was smelling like alcohol and weed. He reminded me of your father Louis and your sister Lois because that is just how they talked when they got drunk." I was totally surprised because I knew he really wasn't a heavy drinker, the man had to get drunk to approach my Mother with his weak ass explanation as to why he abused her all these years.

It was just the guilt and fear he felt at the thought of his ass going to jail which prompted him to finally come and talk to you. He knew that he received that letter from Beck that put his ass on notice to come up with proof you sold him your house, and he couldn't. It truly hurt me to of found out that strong young man that I grew to love and respect had fell to such a degree. His sudden, come to Jesus moment to now reach out to my Mother after all these years of abusing her, in a failed attempt to win favor or sympathy from her was just the act of a scared cowardly man that knew he was about to be publicly exposed as to what and how he had financially abused to his Grandmother.

I harked back to when I was shot in my neck back in the day, I knew the man that shot me, Norse Rayford is his name and his brother, Windale, the driver, and I were best of friends up until the night of the shooting. I didn't get a visit from that coward while I was in the hospital nor did I hear from him when I got out of the hospital, they knew where I lived. It wasn't until a day or two before I was to appear in court to testify against him that he came to my job to make a plea to me to not to testify against his ass and put him in jail, and that was a year plus after the shooting. It would be funny if it the two situations were not so serious, here he, Norse, chose to become this big-gangster, shooting up the town not caring who he maimed or killed. Then we have Terrol, choosing to be this big-time real-estate swindler, targeting a helpless 83 year old, not caring if his grandmother suffers in his pursuit to become the owner of a prime piece of real-estate that never belonged to him. They both wimped out at the last minute, begging for forgiveness when it was time to face the Music. What happened to those Big-Balls they were slinging around the town before the judgment day was fast approaching?

ACT-24

Arthur

———∿∿∿———

During the months following the tyrant Terrol threw on my Mother about her consulting my lawyer and the discovery of that last loan he took out, my Mother became very uncomfortable being around him, because he and his mother where giving her the silent treatment. She wasn't afraid that he would do something to her, she just didn't know what to expect next from them.

I took comfort in knowing that David would on 3 or 4 nights of the week stay with her until 9 or 10 o'clock before he would have to go to work. When I would talk to her over the phone she would often ask me, "Bernard, when do you think Terrol will add my name back on title so I can get my tub and get back up to my bedroom?, I'm so tired of sleeping on this hospital bed, and Arthur, (is what she call her Arthritis) won't leave me alone). I would tell her that she would have to just pray that he would do the right thing by her soon. I knew in my heart that he was never going to help her I just didn't want to say that to her.

127

My Mother's fear about her not knowing but thinking about what Terrol would do next was well founded. It is just remarkable the extent or depth of the callousness and greed in which that mother/son team, Geraldine/Terrol, went to in order to secure sole possession of my Mother's home. Instead of them coming to me, knowing what I was trying to achieve, and it didn't even have to be me, they could have went to J.D., Lois or Donna, and said, (lets all put our funds together and come up with enough money to get Mother the tub and lift she needs.) But no, that would have been too much like the right thing to do. Their brilliant idea was to pool their resources and hire a lawyer to fight their mother/grandmother to keep her house which ended up being the same amount,if not more money it would have taken to help my Mother.

They would rather have confined and condemned my Mother to her dinning room, in sorrow and pain for the rest of her life for just a few $100,000. The ironic thing about their thinking is that they already had possession of the home all I was asking is that they added her to the title so she could get well, and live the rest of her life in comfort, but no, they wanted it all and were so greedy they didn't even want to repay the State for paying for what my Mother needed! There has to be another word for the kind of people that would commit such acts against a helpless Elderly woman, especially their own mother/grandmother, but the Webster Dictionary has yet to come up with it, until such time, I'll just use the word, (Vile!)

All I could do was continue to search online for a portable walk-in tub that I could fit in the kitchen or dinning room area because it had become clear I was on my own in this matter. I found a few tubs but they were manufactured overseas and they were not U.S. compatible unless we converted the pluming in the kitchen or the sink in the restroom off the kitchen adding considerable cost to an already expensive unit. I found a few and the prices ranged from $7-$8,000, plus shipping which was well out of my reach. Another challenge was to find one small enough to fit in that already cluttered dinning room. This situation was beginning to take a heavy toll on me because I could not see a way to get my Mother what she needed and she wasn't getting any better.

ACT-25

Year 2014

*M*y Mother was 93 years young and approaching her 94th birthday, April 29th 2014. Every since her 80th birthday, which was not only her birthday, but it also was the first of two celebrations for her, the second one being her 90th. You see, my Mother was not just my Mother and the Matriarch of the Johnson family, she was a Pillar of the community.

In 2000 she turned 80 years old and a celebration was thrown for her spearheaded by non-other than her daughter, Geraldine. It turned out to be not only a family affair but it became a major event with over 200 friends and relatives in attendance coming from 5 different states, Washington, California, Denver, Detroit, and Oklahoma, to honor my Mother.

The birthday celebration of 2000 that Geraldine and her trusty side-kick, Debra, pulled off for our mother was a huge success and won the undying appreciation and trust of my Mother. The 90th celebration too was a success although it was only a 3rd of the turnout for various reasons. One reason being that my Mother had out lived many of her friends and some of the family that attended the first one, including 3 of her sons/grandson, plus a lot of things change in the course of 10 years. Geraldine had the talent to pull off events such as these and had she pursued and sharpened her skills in that area early on in her life she could have been a successful Party Planner and perhaps left a legacy for her own children, rather than having to swindle her mother out of her house.

My Mother's birthday was always a special day for the family but, after her 80th it took on more significance and became like the extra Holiday of the year. She continued cooking and baking well into her late 80's and on her birthdays she would prepare either a large breakfast or a large dinner for the day. More often than not Geraldine would be there to assist her in that process. She would be the one that would clean and straighten up the house getting it ready for the family and guest, setting the dining room table and make sure Mother had everything in order, while giving orders to the rest of us as to where to sit at the table, she loved the art of delegating and taking charge, as I said, I think she missed her true calling.

This tradition continued through 2014 and it was unfortunately the last one and was not sponsored by Geraldine but the celebration went on. The most astonishing twist to the conspiracy Geraldine and her son Terrol had put in play was that they had to pretend to care about her siblings, laughing, talking, and engaging with them for the better part of 10 years while all the time plotting to take everybody's inheritance, they just couldn't wait to drop the hammer on them once my Mother died.

At the end of April 2014 Geraldine reluctantly flew up for my Mother's 94th birthday but this time it was in a very different capacity. She flew in town unannounced a few days before my Mother's birthday and after pulling up in front of the house, she and her daughter walked up to come in the house. When they walked in Mother and I were sitting in the living room watching, of course, The Price Is Right on the tube. It would be funny if it wasn't so sad, but when they walked in my Mother was sitting in her lounge chair and I on the coach, they both just turned to her and stood right in front of her, not even acknowledging me, with their backs to me, said a few words to her and then just walked out. What the fuck was that?!!! She hadn't seen her mother for a year and she spent less than 5 minutes with her. They saw how frail my Mother was but never bothered to ask how she was doing and never considered offering her any help, they just promptly left the house and probably went straight downtown to pay their attorney some more money. The fact of the matter is that the only reason Geraldine flew to Portland that day was because she had purchased her ticket several months earlier and it was nonrefundable, she really didn't want to be there.

Furthermore unlike in years passed, she didn't partake in planning the dinner, she didn't arrange the dinning room table, and she didn't walk around the house the day of the dinner trying to be the life of the party and shouting out giving orders to everybody as she so loved doing. This was because she knew the cat was out of the bag and she could no longer walk among us faking as if she cared about us, her credibility and station with the family plummeted, including with our Mother. The day before the dinner was to take place we all got together to plan the menu. Geraldine was never shunned by any of my siblings, it was her decision to not be there during the planning of the meal that was to be served which really didn't come as a surprise to my siblings because she hadn't talk to any of them for over 7 months before flying to Portland. So that evening, Lois, and her partner Phyllis, went home to their kitchen, David went home to his kitchen, and Bernita went home to her's. Donna and myself took charge of Mother's kitchen, Geraldine was nowhere in sight.

Our Mother was a bit nervous that we wouldn't be able to pull it off on such short notice. But by 4 o'clock that afternoon the dinning room was set up with all the China and Silver ware in place on the table, the house was in order and the dinner was prepared and we were ready for the guess to arrive.

David came to the house about noon-ish with a huge pot of greens & ham hocks, Lois cooked and brought a large pot of sweet potatoes and, Phyllis baked and brought a large honey ham, they came to the house at about 1:30. With Donna assisting me and with Mother's guidance, we baked two large pans of turkey wings and gravy with dressing and a large pan of mac & cheese which we had ready at about 3 o'clock. Bernita walked in at about 3:30 with the large bowl of banana pudding that she made and two pies she purchased from Albertson's, lemon & pecan.

We not only pulled it off, we knocked it out of the park. It turned out to be a beautiful presentation and a wonderful Happy Birthday dinner for our Mother, despite a few haters wishing for us to fail. Shortly thereafter family and guest began arriving the first to arrive was Geraldine, her daughter and co-conspirators, Arleta, and of course, Ms. Debra was right behind her. When they entered the house I was standing in the living room talking to my uncle JD and my Mother, the three of them greeted my Mother, kissing and wishing her happy birthday, but Geraldine and Arleta said nothing to my uncle or myself. On the other hand Debra came in with her usual vibrant self, acknowledged all of us with that beautiful wide smile of her's. She had nothing to do with what was going on within the family, she is just one of Geraldine's loyal followers and a beautiful person. Geraldine then just strolled through the dinning room and kitchen where Donna, Lois, Bernita and Phyllis were all sitting, as she glancing at the beautiful layout on the table that she thought couldn't be done without her. All of them greeted her with respect as she passed through doing her inspection even though she was not being her vibrant, effervescent self. With class, Lois, Donna, Phyllis, and David still welcomed her and her guess, they were not going to allow her to dampen that day for our Mother, Geraldine and her cronies hung around for a while mostly out on the porch, not engaging in the festivities with the family, she stayed just long enough to bless the meal, she lead the prayer, then they left, not eating a bite. It was obvious to all that she was uncomfortable being there not being in her usual, self appointed leadership role. Her swift departure from the house did nothing to diminish the joyful festivities because the guest continued arriving with greetings and baring gifts to honor my Mother's birthday. Actually her leaving the party was not the most interesting non-event of the day that award went to her son Terrol, he never showed his face all that day, he stayed upstairs through the whole celebration, go figure. It wasn't until the last of the guess had left and while Donna, Lois, David, and I were cleaning up the kitchen, putting away what little leftovers there were, that he eased down the stairs and on his way out the door paused for a second and said to our Mother, "happy birthday grandma" then turned and walked out, not saying anything to either of us. The fact that he stayed up in his room the whole time and his mother made a quick departure from the party just made for a more pleasant day for all involved because the objective was to make sure our Mother had a memorable and joyous 94th Birthday celebration with no drama and we accomplished that.

As Donna and I were straightening out the dinning room getting it ready for Mother so she could get to that hospital bed for the night, as she was in her lounge chair sleeping, Donna said to me, "You know Bernard I kind a felt sorry for Geraldine today, she seemed to be so out of place" I had to remind her, I said, " Donna, listen, Geraldine and Terrol have over the years morphed themselves into being heartless, greedy, narcissists mutants, and for ten years conspired to take from everybody in this family, including our Mother no matter who they hurt along the way, the problem for them is that they got caught because time ran out on them.

She didn't fly up here to make things right with our Mother even after seeing with her own eyes how much pain and suffering she was going through and couldn't get around without assistance. She could have told Terrol the day she got here, son we have to put mother back on title with you, today so she can get the tub she needs to soak her body and chronic arthritis. But no, she just smiled in her face and walked out on her. Her behavior was due to fact that she had got outed and the whole family knew and what you seen in her was a woman ashamed and embarrassed, yet with no remorse, so feel sorry for her if you must, she sure don't feel anything for you!"

Needless to say in the subsequent months nothing changed, they just kept paying their lawyer to keep the home solely in Terrol's name, ignoring the needs of my Mother which was more than frustrating to me because I knew that they were not going to help our Mother and I knew too that we still hadn't raised enough money to help her. During those same months my Mother's pain became worse so her doctor prescribed her Norco which is an (opioid) to relieve some of the pain, she was taking as many as 3 or 4 a day. Here was this 94 year old woman who had smoked her last cigarette in 1960 and she never drank and now finds herself trying to function under the influence of narcos. We had to make sure she had a portable toilet next to her at all times because taking those pills made it more challenging for her to get to the restroom. She didn't like the way the pills made her feel so when I came up there at the end of August she told me just that, so we decided to take her off of them.

How Terrol could come in and out of that house each day and not be effected by what he saw her going through the last few years with no plans to help her get up those very stairs to her bedroom, that he climbed everyday to his room, having to pass her to go up them, and also having to pass her bedroom to get to his plush bedroom, while she slept down stairs on a hospital bed is truly amazing. The man had been salivating for years in anticipation of calling her large Master Bedroom his own.

ACT-26

We'll Be Missing You

Shortly after I left Portland on or about the 3rd of September of 2014, another sad trip driving back home leaving my Mother. But this time I felt a bit better because I knew that we had convinced her to go to the doctor and get cortisone shots in her knees to relieve the excruciating pain from her chronic arthritis, she really didn't want to do it, but my brother David took her to her appointment a few days after I left. I called her a few days later to see how she was feeling and I was pleasantly surprised, she told me that she hadn't felt that good in recent memory. She was getting around much better and sounding better as well, the shots were working, but not enough that she could get up to bathtub or to her bedroom. We continued to talk on a daily bases and she felt well enough to attend church services, so David escorted her two Sundays in a row in September. It wasn't but a week or so later, on the 24th or 25th, David called me and told me that our Mother was in the hospital with pneumonia once again and that I needed to get up there because the doctors said she was giving up and rejecting treatment.

That was one of the saddest days of my life because I knew then that she was tired. Why she caught pneumonia again I don't know, but what I do know is that she was still sleeping next to that cold ass window every night instead of being upstairs in her warm bedroom where she should and could have been for the last couple of years of her life had Terrol and his mother Geraldine had her wellbeing in mind!!

I got on the freeway to Portland on the on the 26th of September, I met with David that Night and when I arrived and we went straight to the hospital to see her. When we walked in her room she was just lying there calm and motionless while family members surrounded her bed, I approached her and put her hands in mine and kissed her, I knew then she was leaving me. I stayed only a few minutes because Geraldine and Terrol were among the family members that was there and I couldn't stand to be in the same room with those two because I was afraid of what I might say or do to them, so I left. Later that night I returned and sat with her and held her hands, and talked to her, she had beautiful hands. In that moment I noticed and focused on them, I realized then where I got my hands from, only larger. As I sat and talked to her, she was unresponsive but I felt she knew I was there, I sat there with her for a couple of hours. I then went back to the house to get some rest because I hadn't slept since being in the town. I really couldn't sleep so I got up a couple hours later got dressed and headed back to the hospital to see her. And half way there Donna called me crying and said that the nurse had just called her to tell her that our Mother had just passed away. I had to pull over and gather myself, I knew it was coming but the reality that it had happened hit me like a shockwave to the head because I wanted to be there with her at that time, so now again I wasn't there for her. It was as if she was just waiting on me to come and talk to her before she crossed over to be with her Lord and savior.

After pulling myself together I continued to the hospital. Upon walking in to the room the fear of knowing then I'm about to see my Mother in the state of death something just came all over my body, it was as if her spirit was still in the room, because it had only been less than an hour that they pronounced her dead and when I looked over at her lying there motionless but with a since of piece on her face, it just tore me up. I approached her and sat next to her and again reached over and put her hands in mine, and the first thing I noticed was that see had a tear drop on the edge of each of her eyes.

I then took the tissue off the night stand and dabbed the tears off of her eyes and began shedding tears of my own while holding her close to me. After about 45 minutes or so Geraldine and Terrol walked into the room and when they entered I was still holding my Mother's, hands, they walked to the far side of her bed and stood over her. I saw no emotion or a tear from either of them, it was just, matter of fact to them. I couldn't stay in there with them because I was about to say to them (" Well I guess you two finally got what ya'll wanted, she's dead now and the house is now yours") So I just left thinking that was not the time or place but in hine-site I feel now I should have just let them have it right then.

I left the hospital and drove a few miles to one of my sons mother's house, Elnora Scarborough, to tell her that Mother had past, she just reached out and hugged me in tears, then we sat and talked about it. She lost her mother to cancer several years earlier so she could feel my pain and she knew what I was going through. So I sat there with her and her brother George for a few minutes then I asked her for a few dollars so I could go to my friends house who had a bar stocked with liqueur to get something to drink, she gave me a few hundred and I left. I went straight to his house and bought a fifth of Crown Royal from him and then drove to the house and began drinking. After an hour or two had passed Terrol walked in the door, he had no words for me, nor did I have any for him, right then. So after downing half of that fifth I decided to gather up the things I wanted that belonged to my Mother so I could get out of that town before I lost it and did something I would regret. It wasn't much, I took a blanket that she slept with, and I took her Bible. I them went upstairs to her bedroom and there was this Mink like bedspread that I seen in her room for a couple of years or so, and I assumed it was her's, so I folded it up and took it down to my car to put it in the trunk of my car. As I was doing so, Terrol walked out the door and told me that the bedspread was his.

Those were the first words out of that man's mouth, to me, in well over 6 months. He was concerned about a bedspread, so I took it back to my Mother's Bedroom. As I was leaving her room he was standing there in the door way of his room, I just couldn't hold it anymore, so I said. "So I guess you and your mother are satisfied now, my Mother is dead so you now own her house just as you planned, you'll just couldn't wait for this day!". And then I went on to ask him, "did you buy it from her?" he turned and walked off. Then I asked him about the monies my Mother and I was giving him each month over all those years, he just dismissed it as if it didn't count for anything and it wasn't going towards the house payments, it was just something else we were doing. So I replied, ("Nigga, what do you mean, something else? So according to you, I was just giving you money, huh? So you and your Bitch ass mama, stole my Mother's money and her home?!") he then lunged at me as if he was about to swing on me, I said ("Oh so you are going to beat me up now, huh?") then he froze, caught his self and said to me, (" I want you out of this house, now!") I told him ("Oh, Mother Fucker I'm leaving this house but not because you are demanding I do,

I'm leaving to avoid a homicide up in here! But I'm not leaving until I bury my Mother and Fuck you! That man just don't know how close he was to getting shot that very night, my Mother's body was still warm and he was trying to put me out of her house, the house I was raised in! Trust me, anybody else would have killed that man, then and there, I'm just not a killer.

I was planning on leaving anyway when I sobered up and drive back home to Sacramento see about my family. I had no intention of being around those people awaiting my Mother's funeral especially in the state of mind I was in.

The man wanted me out my Mother's house the very night she died, and said it! Now that is some bold ass shit to say to a man the night that he just lost his Mother. He knew the house was in his name and there was nothing I could do about it. He was now in full control, the perfect crime had been committed, and now in place. Now I'm thinking to myself, (I'm going to shoot this Nigga!) But what I did instead was went down stairs and looked around the house for what else I wanted of my Mother's to take home with me and glanced towards the dining room window and noticed the plants that she had in that windows for years. She would sometimes ask me to water them when I came up to see her. This one plant had grown to be about 3 or 4 feet over the years she had it. The plant is some strain of Philodendron, so I gently untwined it from the window seal and just as gently placed it in the back seat of my car. Afterwards I went back into the house and knocked off the remainder of that fifth Of Crown Royal and cried myself to sleep on that fucked up ass hospital bed that my Mother was forced to sleep on to in some way to feel her. The next morning Lois came by the house and convinced me to stay a day or two to help pick out Mother's casket with my siblings, Geraldine included, that was real tuff on me to have to sit there with her even for that short period of time.

At the break of dawn the day after we picked out our Mother's casket I got on the freeway back to Sacramento. And again the drive back was one of pure sadness thinking about the Matriarch of the Johnson family was no longer here and also thinking about how she must have felt over the last years of why and how she was so disrespected by her daughters and grandson. Then again I was also thinking that my Mother is now with her Maker, in his House now, no more pain, no more suffering, in a strange way I felt happy for her, but it draws me to tears every time I think about how they did her. There is no plus side to this but if there was it would be that I no longer had to worry about how they would be treating her while I was away from her. The down side to that thinking is that the reality of me not ever hearing my Mother's beautiful voice or ever seeing her beautiful face again just boggles my mind! It was the toughest ride back to Sacramento out of all the years prior.

Once I pulled up to the house I unpacked the car, went in and laid down and slept for hours, I didn't realize how tired I was. The next morning I woke up and went to the corner store and purchased some Folgers coffee and bread and when I returned home I went into the kitchen and brewed some coffee for two and put some toast in the oven. My Mother loved her toast and coffee in the mornings, I grew up with that smell as a kid. I pretended she was there and I sat in front of the television and watched her favorite daytime shows as we did every morning together over many years, tears flowing.

Later that afternoon I then looked for the proper place to set her plant, it was only one spot that was appropriate and it was in the corner of my living room near the window so I could raise it to the window seal and over the window as she had it in her dinning room. It reached only about half way across my front window. That's where it has been sitting for the last four years and it is thriving.

144

A few days later I drove back up to Portland to attend my Mother's funeral which turned out to be an event, more so than just a funeral. She filled her church with family, friends, and well wishers. It was held at the (Life Change Church) in north Portland, where she became a member a few years earlier, because the church she belonged to before had a flight of stairs she could no longer climb.

It was standing room only and she had three Pastors speaking at the service, the Pastor of her Church, Pastor Strong, Reverend Pack, a long time friend of the family, and her son-in-law, Pastor Gardner. And of course they all spoke very highly of her and Praised her for all the good she brought to the Community, the Church, and to the Eastern Star Organization. Pastor Gardner said a few words and some of those words were directed straight at me. He stood up there and looked me dead in my eyes and said, ('Your Mother, Mrs. Lucille, did what she did, for all of you") as if he was telling me that he knew how his wife, Geraldine and her son Terrol had violated my Mother's wishes.

I haven't talked to him, Terrol, or his wife Geraldine since that day. I also have a brother and two sisters still living in Portland just blocks away, and neither one of them have stepped into that house since that week, and I haven't since that day!

My Mother was laid to rest in the most respectable fashion fitting to her long time here on this earth and in keeping with the way in which she carried herself with the, Character, Courage, and Pride she exuded throughout her Long Exemplary life. My Mother was a woman that prepared herself for any eventuality, financially, but what she couldn't anticipate was that her own children would prevent her from living her last years in comfort as she had planned. If there were such a thing as a National Data Base for people that lived all of their lives doing the right thing, work hard, buy a home, raise their children, had no enemies, never been arrested, and live to be 94 years or more, my

Mother could have been a spoke person, and or a poster woman for such a organization. That proud woman did everything right, she treated people with respect regardless of their station in life. She took joy and pride in satisfying peoples pallets with her original style of Soul Food cooking all of her adult life.

It wasn't until she reached the age 84 that her world began turning on her from within her own domain. In my life experience I learned that a person can do everything right in life and shit can still go wrong.

I too learned that a person can do so much for another that the person on the receiving end might feel some kind of way because they feel they can't ever be able to repay it, and in some cases they can grow contempt towards the giver. I know in my Mother's life time she too seen her share of people mistreating one another, people fighting and taking from each other, even hating each other. Never in her wildest dreams did she think any of that kind of behavior would hit so close to home, let alone towards her, by her own children. But the reality is that her home became ground zero for those that chose to target her and turning her into their own Cash Cow to satisfy their thirst for greed at her expense. I have no doubt the Angle my Mother, was and the God fearing woman she was, she saw it in her heart to forgive those that trespassed against her and that she would want me to do the same, " I'm sorry Mother, I Love you, but that will never happen!"

Jesus only had one Judas in his flock, my Mother raised and had three in her's, she had no chance. I think back on my Mother's situation and I see how it was pure greed that was the reason her daughters, Bernita, Geraldine and grandson, Terrol felt the need to take that Beautiful woman through years of pain and suffering. Greed can be considered nefarious, because it causes people to commit acts so outrageous that it becomes incomprehensible. I just have to say this about Terrol and his mom Geraldine, yes, they ended up with my Mother's home as they planned, but no matter what other accomplishments they may achieve going forward, this is still a hollow victory because its was ill gotten and they didn't achieve it on their own merits, they had to pray somebody died to get it, and it was at the expense of my Mother's life. And no matter how they may appear to the public, trust me, it has to be haunting them. Then again, maybe not, because most narcissist have no compassion, or regret for what pain they cause to others. But in cases like this, no matter what, they will still be walking around town with the stench of Shit that will forever be on their shoes.

Unfortunately my sister Bernita won't be around any longer for people smell the stench on her shoes, because she has since passed away. I say unfortunately because I didn't want her to die but I felt so much contempt for her, because it was she that put in motion the eventual events that put my Mother in peril. And I harbor the same sentiments for Geraldine and Terrol, not for death, or even prison, because that's not how I roll. But I did wish for all of them to live long miserable lives and get a (Healthy Dose) of what it was like to live years in fear, pain, suffering, uncertainty, and betrayal, and not being able the bathe their asses for years, just as they put my Mother through. None of those weak parasites would not be able to survive half as long as my Mother did under those circumstances.

There was an amazingly ridiculous statement made by a member of the family, whose name I won't mention, they know who they are, (Rolonda) Oops! she said. " well I guess God wanted Bernita to come and be with her Mother" Really?! I guarantee you, Bernita could not ever get anywhere near to the gates where my Mother is, let alone get passed them.

EBONY AND SONS

Epilogue

————ɱ————

*A*llow me to tell you just how (Bad-Ass) Mrs. Lucille Johnson was. This Icon of a woman bore 10 children, raised 6 of them all on her own! She fed, clothed and educated all of them except one, and thats only because Susie Mae passed away at an early age. This academically challenged woman worked her ass off to provide for her children and that was her main focus in life. Out of 9 of her educated off springs only one of them came close to accomplishing what she did, his name was Louis Henry Johnson Jr., her second son. But not even he did it all on his own, as she did, he had a wife that helped him. He joined the military at a young age, married, and had two beautiful grandchildren for our Mother. Then he and his wife went on to purchase a prime piece of real-estate while raising them and then together paid it off. There were only 2 other of her children that purchased homes but none of them kept them long enough to pay them off as did she. My Mother purchased her home at 506 n. e. Skidmore in Portland Oregon in 1962 and paid it off by working hard everyday. In fact there are court documents that suggest she may have even just saved up enough money over the years to have paid a third down for the house only to have three deviants pretending to be loving children come in and take it from her. This strong Black woman survived loosing one daughter, two grandchildren, and in 2008, she also had to bury two of her eldest sons all while under going dialysis treatments three times a week. This strong Beautiful woman at the age 88 year old started undergoing those treatments and continued doing so for over six years until she finally lost her fourth bout with pneumonia at the age of 94 years old. And I'm willing to go out on a limb here and state that this Matriarch of the Johnson family holds the record for a person of her age to be on dialysis for that length of time, and if not, she is in the top ten. My Mother in her last years lived through a crucible and passed with courage, they disrespected her, they broke her heart, and they broke her financially, but they couldn't break her spirit and her belief in her Lord and Savior. My Mother lived a life that deserved respect, admiration, and she should have been revered by all, especially her children/grandchildren. Those that violated her should be throughout their lives marked with shame and disgrace!

There are several things I would love to say to and let my Mother know about what has been happening in her absents but, knowing my Mother she has managed to work her way closer to her God and as a result of that he may have took her under his wings and elevated her to Guardian Angle status, so she probably already know what I want to tell her. Should that be the case she would be aware of the fact that her disrespectful, albatross, of a daughter passed away January of 2017. Also she would know that her most respected, self made, and brutally honest grandson, Earl Johnson, Lois's one and only child too passed away in 2017. And if he makes it to the gates she would no doubt campaign for him to get through them. Unfortunately my sister Lois, the strongest of the Johnson sisters, yet again became the victim of financial Greed by none other than her grandson, DeRay Johnson, Earl's son. After Earl passed (God bless his Sole) Lois and DeRay flew out to the east coast to bury him and take care of his affairs.

Once they arrived they met Earl's, friend and closest confidant and according to him, Earl had confided in him that he was going to leave his car to his mother. He also said that Earl intended to adjust his insurance policy to leave a portion of it to his mother, whom he loved dearly, and DeRay was there as he was explaining this to his mother. And at that time he told his grandmother that he didn't even want the car. But somewhere down the line he change his mind and decided to keep the car for himself. The problem was that Earl's condition declined so rapidly and therefore he couldn't modify his policy, Earl had an estate worth close to, if not more than $100,000.

Sadly DeRay ignored what Earl's friend had just relayed to them and the Greediator again raised his ugly head in the Johnson family. Now Earl's friend had no dog in this fight therefore had no reason to lie, he was just relaying what Earl had said to him in what was comparable to a death bed confession. DeRay decided not share the insurance policy with his grandmother, although my sister Lois looks like she is only 50 years old, that beautiful woman is in her 70's and thereby considered by law Elderly. And maybe DeRay's actions may not constitute Elderly Financially abuse he could have done more, after all, Earl was her only son.

Ok, he end up buying his grandmother a 6 or $7000 car to try and make up for the $30,000 car her son wanted her to have, with the proceeds of his inheritance but that was only to try and make himself free of the guilt of knowing he did not do right by his grandmother. He should have shared that money with her as well, he knew she was struggling and needed money.

If people live long enough they find out in time, (Karma is indeed a Bitch), she visits some people sooner, others she waits until later, but trust me, she is coming, just ask John, and as in DeRay's case, she too visited him sooner as well. That young man was so intoxicated on the thought of having more money than he had ever seen in his 30 plus years of his life. He even neglected to repay his cousin Rolonda for going into her savings or using her credit card so she could finance the flight for him and his mother to go and bury his father. This should have been the first thing he was suppose to do was pay her once he returned. Now 8 months later he didn't even have any money left to do so. My sister Lois couldn't even repay her, and she would have but because he didn't give her any of the money she couldn't.

I just want to say to him, DeRay, and to his cousin or what ever Terrol is to him, and that is, there are multitudes of ways people gain respect in life but, taking or swindling from the Elderly whether it be from a stranger or your own mother/grandmother is not one of those ways. DeRay is young enough to recover and realize that his mother and grandmother are the reason he is in existence and from this day forward take care of them, he will then see his life will be a whole lot more prosperous.

Respect is something that is earned throughout life, you have to actually do something in your life to achieve it, its not just giving to you. I can just see my Mother up there now just shaking her head saying, (they all are just Crooks) those were her favorite word for people living outside of the law.

I have to say and give DeRay a few props, at least he did give his grandmother something, unlike Terrol who didn't give his grandmother a Penny of the thousands he sold from her!

On a more positive note, she would also know that her well educated, yet once fallen granddaughter Ebony, has risen above the deep, dark, place she once found herself in and against with what seem to be insurmountable odds she recapture her former self and in doing so went back to school earning a few State issued certificates, Oregon GED Summit, Higher Education Commission, and a Certificate Recovery Mentorship, from the Board of Oregon and went on to land a prestigious position of employment in a State office. She also proved to the state that she was not only worthy but ready, willing and able to take on the responsibility of taking care of her two sons and that they are all together living well today.

Another thing she would know, if her guardianship extended to my household is that the 4 foot plant she so coveted over the years in her dinning room and had me water so often is thriving and has grown to be close to 30 feet long throughout the sealing of my living room.

From your remaining Loving and Loyal children, Rosizean, Lois, Donna, David, and myself, we Love and Miss You, Big-Time Mother!!!

P. S. In the Lucille Johnson Case in an ironic way I feel a bit responsible because had I went ahead and delivered street justice to my brother Roy by shooting and maiming his ass for what he did to me, as the unwritten code of the streets recommends, that may have served as a deterrent sending a message to Terrol and his mother Geraldine that it might not be such a good idea to do what they planned and done to my Mother.

For The Record

I just want to state, I am not a seasoned writer or a professional novelist, nor do I play one on TV. I'm not anticipating this Biography will hit the New York Times best seller list or seeing myself on a book signing tour for it. The purpose of these writings were just to keep my Mother's memory alive and to expose those that so trespassed against her in such a Loathsome way for financial gain. It has never been about money with me, I just want the readers of these writings to take away from them what is really going on in Portland Oregon and throughout this country and that is Financial Elderly Abuse is on the rise and people should be aware of those that target our mothers/ grandmother/fathers/ grandfathers. My plan is to just order a few hundred copies and pass them out in the City of Portland, free of charge, that would ease my mind immensely knowing my Mother's story is being told!

The repetition of my Mother's condition and her life prolonging needs throughout these writings was by Design.

She was a Great Woman!!! This biography of Lucille Johnson and the other examples of Financial Abuse within doesn't even scratch the surface of the ongoing abuse of this kind throughout this country. The examples of Financial Elderly Abuse stated here in was mostly in n. e. Portland, in a 10 mile radios. I would like for anyone that reads this and have Elderly love ones to reach out to them and check on them on a regular basis because you never know who or what is lurking around them if you don't ask. Had I listen to my friend and or paid closer attention early on there would have been a different outcome then what happened to my Mother.

Acknowledgments

━━━∿∿∿━━━

I would be remiss of me to not mention two of the most dearest and spiritual non-Biological Women that were in my Mother's life.

I would like to thank Ms. Diane Scott for her being there for my Mother in times of need throughout the many years they knew each other. Diane's mother, Sister Scott too was a dear friend of my Mother, in fact she being the wonderful and caring woman she was she reached out and took in one of my Mother's grandchildren, raised and educated him when his mother, Geraldine couldn't, my Mother was forever grateful to her for her generosity and compassion for doing so.

Some years later Diane too showed her generosity that she no doubt inherited from her Mother when she reached out and helped my sister Bernita when she lost her son, (Trapper) in a shooting at a young age. Just to be clear, that beautiful and caring woman didn't do it for Bernita, she did it out of pure Love for my Mother! But she did hold Bernita for the debt and I'm not sure if she ever got all of her money back from her, but she never asked my Mother for any of it!

I have to say this about Ms. Diane Scott, I think she had planned all along to get her hands on my Mother's secret recipe for her signature Peach Cobbler as well, and she got it. (Lol)!

The other Beautiful Woman I want to mention is another Diane that my Mother met some 30 years before she passed, Diane Sentell, her daughter-in-Law and the mother of my beautiful Daughter. Diane not only raised and educated our daughter and her son Bill, she also took in and helped me raise and educate two of my sons, Anwar and Bernard. She and my Mother became very close friends and spiritual confidants. They would talk on the phone on a weekly, if not daily basis, they would talk about the kids, they would talk about their Day-time Soaps, and of course they would talk about me.

She and my Mother were both God fearing and Religious Souls and they also prayed together over the phone constantly and I'm sure they are up there now praying for me, knowing I need it, Big-Time, I miss them both so much!

These two Dianes did more for my Mother in the last years of her life than her own biological daughter Geraldine. She was paying a lawyer to help her son Terrol keep my Mother's home a property he didn't pay a dime for, knowing my Mother needed money and assistance. But these two women stayed in touch with my Mother, constantly, praying with her, keeping her spirits up during the most trying times of her life when her own daughter had betrayed her. And in doing so, they were never expecting anything in return, they just Loved her. I'll be forever grateful to those two Beautiful women!

There is this age old question, is a person better off in life to have had love and lost, or to have never had love at all? This same question can also be asked about money. Coming from one that has had an abundance of both for years, I would have to say, personally, and without question, I would rather have had!

Love You Mother!!!

57743683R00093

Made in the USA
Columbia, SC
13 May 2019